TALES
of
FAITH

TALES *of* FAITH

A Guide to Sharing the Gospel through Literature

HOLLY ORDWAY

WORD on FIRE INSTITUTE

Published by the Word on Fire Institute, an imprint of
Word on Fire, Park Ridge, IL 60068

Printed in the United States of America

Cover design, typesetting, and interior art direction
by Cassie Bielak, Marlene Burrell, and Rozann Lee.

25 24 23 22 1 2 3 4

ISBN: 978-1-685780-12-8

Library of Congress Control Number: 2021922719

To my students: past, present, and future

CONTENTS

Chapter One
LEADING WITH BEAUTY

Welcome to our journey!

As Christians, we are called to invite others to know and love our Lord Jesus Christ and to become part of his Body, the Church. How can literature assist us in this work of evangelization, catechesis, and discipleship? It is helpful to articulate this role more fully, so that we can have a clear and confident sense of *why* and *how* literature will help us share the faith.

It is challenging to share the Gospel in a culture that dismisses our faith as irrelevant, condemns it as harmful and irrational, or sidelines it as nothing more than personal opinion. Today, many people are resistant to even the most basic claims of Christianity, unwilling to consider it as a real possibility. Many others are only nominally Christian, identifying themselves as having faith but neither understanding nor abiding by the teaching of the Church.

There is no silver bullet, no magic wand that we can wave to solve the problem, nor should we expect that to be the case: people are complex, and so is culture. We are formed by countless influences over the course of our lives, and the culture we live in is made up of many elements – some positive, some negative; many of them contradictory; varying from place to place. In order to share the faith in this strange new world that we live in, we must attend to both evangelization and formation in a holistic way: attending to the whole person, and heeding the needs and questions of each individual. Our efforts must include pastoral care, personal witness, and education; we must attend to intellectual, spiritual, emotional, relational, and physical needs.

Or to put it differently: since God is himself perfect Truth, perfect Goodness, and perfect Beauty, we can and must show people that their intellect, their moral sense, and their longing for beauty can only be fulfilled in a relationship with God through his Church. Since all three transcendentals are united in God, each one, if faithfully followed, leads to the other two.

We can't convey the reality of goodness, truth, and beauty by rational argument alone – that will just leave us making arguments about words and definitions, all very abstract and with little impact on our listeners' hearts, minds, or wills. One of the challenges of evangelization and discipleship, then, is to find ways to invest our Christian concepts with real substance. When words like *grace, forgiveness, sin, resurrection*, and so on have real meaning for people, the questions "Could this be true?" and "How does this affect the way I live my life?" become significant.

One particular example from my own experience stands out. Years ago, when I was teaching at a secular community college in Southern California, I used Shakespeare's play *Macbeth* in my literature and composition classes. In class, we discussed how Macbeth, a brave man who was respected and honored by his king, yielded to the temptation of ambition and became caught in a downward spiral of continued violence, leading to his own destruction. This rather dark and weird play allowed me to discuss issues of sin, temptation, and virtue with an audience of largely unchurched young people, in a context where it would not have been appropriate (or useful) for me to be explicitly Christian in my presentation of these ideas. After our last discussion, the students handed in their homework and filed out of the classroom. As I sorted through the papers, I noticed a sticky note on the back of the stack, which read: "Dr. O: last night I was out with some friends and I was tempted to do something I shouldn't do. But I thought of Macbeth, and I didn't do it."

That was all. I never knew who wrote the note, or what the situation had been, only that there was a student in my class who, at least on one occasion, recognized and resisted sin *because of the imaginative engagement with it in literature* that we had in class. It might seem a small matter, from a certain perspective, but in reality, the movement of a soul away from sin (however small the step) and toward the good (however dimly perceived) is profoundly important.

Stories provide a way to get past barriers of hostility and faulty assumptions, and in particular, the distance provided by *old* stories creates a valuable comfort zone, a sense of safety in considering ideas that, if true, have the alarming potential to change everything in one's life. The very strangeness of the world of Beowulf or Odysseus makes it easier to discuss their actions and attitudes in terms of virtue and vice, objective good and evil. People who are ready to mock or dismiss Christian ideas if these are presented directly are often willing to lower their barriers of hostility and consider where their assumptions might be faulty, if we go about it indirectly and gently through the discussion of stories that are fascinating in their own right.

The meaning-making power of literature is particularly important for catechesis and discipleship, especially for our young people. We cannot take for granted, for instance, that those who are preparing for the sacrament of Confirmation have any real grasp of the faith – even when they have parents who are regular Mass-goers. In my experience, middle-school and high-school students often have only the most superficial understanding of the meaning of words like *prayer* or *sin*. If prayer means just asking God for what you want, and prayer is only 'answered' if you get exactly what you ask for, what happens when a young person prays earnestly that his beloved grandmother recover from illness . . . and she dies? A situation like this is often precisely the point at which a young person walks away from the faith. Similarly, if sin is just an abstract negative label for various activities (mostly sexual, and which the wider culture warmly endorses), the concept provides no meaningful barrier against slipping into sin and into a habitual disregard for the teachings of the Church.

Literature can help the truths of the faith to be more fully assimilated by the imagination, grasped by the intellect, and felt by the emotions – all of which, in turn, helps build a solid foundation for the action of the will.

Leading with beauty means starting with the basic fact that human beings are drawn toward what is beautiful. It attracts us, compels our attention, and if we *stay* attentive to it, we can be drawn further in. Where does this beauty come from, why does it move me, how can I find more of it? These are questions that lead us toward God and, especially with the help of an evangelist or a catechist, can help us to know and love him more.

Leading with beauty can take many forms. This book attends specifically to literature; that is, stories, poetry, and drama. These forms, whether written down or passed along by the spoken word, have been a meaningful part of human existence for as long as we have recorded history. As soon as we have writing, we have evidence of storytelling and poetry. And, ancient as it is, literature is as vibrant today as it has ever been – bursting out into new forms and media, but also thriving in the 'old-school' form of printed books. This book particularly focuses on ancient and medieval literature – precisely because this literature, of very great age, allows us to focus much more clearly on the essential questions of the human experience, and to see these issues with fresh eyes.

The approach of this book

This book has two complementary purposes. First, it provides a resource for teachers, catechists, ministry leaders, and parents who are seeking to foster spiritual conversations that are inviting, enriching, and nonthreatening, and to find fresh ways to engage students with core Christian teaching in meaningful ways. The literary texts covered here provide a safe arena for engaging with important questions in a nonthreatening way, and they help readers build up a greater sense of meaning for the elements of our faith. Second, this book is a guide for individual readers to explore great literature, reflect on it in meaningful ways, and be better prepared to share their faith and help others to grow in their faith. In this way, *Tales of Faith* provides a framework both for evangelization of those on the peripheries of the Church – 'nones,' seekers, skeptics, fallen-away Catholics – and for discipleship and catechesis of those who are part of the family of faith.

The selections included in this guide do not exhaust the possibilities of literary texts that can be used very fruitfully for outreach, discipleship, and personal formation. Far from it! As you can see, I've chosen to focus only on ancient and medieval literature. The selections are such that as you move through the whole book, you'll gain a sense of the possibilities of using literature in evangelization and discipleship. You'll become more well-rounded as a reader, and this will expand your options as an evangelist, catechist, or teacher. And from that foundation, I hope that you'll find even more tales of faith – or write them yourself! – to share with a world starved for the beauty, truth, and goodness of Christianity.

What's inside?

The texts discussed here come from the ancient through the late medieval period, starting with Greek mythology and ending with Dante's *Divine Comedy*. I've deliberately chosen to limit the chronological range (though, as it is, we still cover thousands of years!) for two practical reasons: first, it keeps the book at a manageable length; and second, these are periods for which I have extensive teaching experience.

Within each chapter are sections focusing on a single text, and each section has five parts:

First, each section begins with a short ***Introduction*** that draws out a few key themes and ideas that are relevant for evangelization, catechesis, and discipleship.

Since all of these works are so rich that entire books could be (and have been) written about them, the essays don't try to be comprehensive in what they cover. Rather, I've drawn on my own experience in teaching literature to highlight certain aspects that open the door to productive engagement with the material. My aim is to *suggest* and *invite*, and to model ways of thinking about and discussing literature that encourage readers, students, and discussion participants to go deeper and explore further on their own. I do *not* include a summary of the work (at most, I offer a brief recap to provide context for the rest of the discussion).

Next, each section features a ***Selection*** from a translation of the text; in some cases, the full text of a story or poem is included. For longer works, I have chosen an excerpt that provides a taste of that work, so that you can decide whether or not to read the full text on your own. The excerpts are chosen to stand on their own to a certain extent, and to correspond with at least some of the themes noted in the Introduction for that text, so as to be suitable for use in teaching and discussion-leading. I have always chosen the excerpts from an edition in the public domain, even when it's not the best translation. Teachers, therefore, can freely duplicate and share the excerpts with their classes without any further permissions needed. See *Recommended Resources* for my suggestions about the best editions for each text if you plan to go beyond the selected section. The material following each Selection is intended to support the use of this book for evangelization, catechesis, and formation.

Recommended Resources – These include suggested editions of the books under discussion, as well as supporting material and further reading. Every text that I've included here is readily accessible, either in print or in e-text form, and all of them have translations that are in the public domain. Most of them also have modern editions that are inexpensive and easy to find. As a result, you can use this guide to develop reading lists for book groups, homeschools, parish programming, and so on without having to worry about sourcing obscure or expensive texts.

Questions for Discussion – These questions are suitable for immediate use in a group discussion; they can serve as a guide for the discussion leader or as a handout for the whole group, and can be adapted into writing assignments as well. The audience envisioned for these questions is that of interested high school students and above. All of these questions assume a clear, basic understanding of the text itself; for high school or early college students, especially those without much practice in reading, I recommend that the teacher or discussion leader add in a few comprehension questions at the start. The more in-depth questions can also be used as prompts for writing activities. These questions are primarily intended to support study in groups (classes, families, discussion groups, and so on), but they are beneficial to self-guided readers as well.

Using the Arts – These are hands-on activities for small groups, drawing on literature, the visual arts, music, and drama to help participants engage meaningfully with the concepts covered in that selection. As written, the activities are intended for use with grade school through college-age students. Note that for the visual arts, some museums, such as the UK National Gallery, allow free downloads for personal use; many images are also available in the public domain on Wikimedia Commons.

Chapter Two

PREPARING FOR OUR LITERARY JOURNEY

This book is a guide for a journey through ancient and medieval literature, and as with any journey, there will be challenges along the way! In particular, since this book is specifically aimed at supporting evangelization and discipleship, readers should be prepared for a certain amount of spiritual warfare. You *will* find difficulties in the journey; the only question is what the challenges will be, and how well prepared you, and the groups you lead or teach, are to face them.

Using vs. receiving literature

Although this book has a practical purpose, I wish to emphasize at the start the importance of encountering literature on its own terms: as an experience that we enter into, and as something that we receive as a good in itself, not merely something that we use for other ends, however laudable. As J.R.R. Tolkien put it, "We make in our measure and in our derivative mode, because we are made: and not only made, but made in the image and likeness of a Maker."[1] The impulse to create stories and to respond to them is a basic part of being human. My aim is to model an approach to literature that engages both the intellect and the imagination, and that allows us to use these works for evangelization and discipleship, while also preserving and fostering appreciation and enjoyment of them as literature.

That's why we need to be careful never to take a utilitarian approach. If we treat literature as a mere tool to achieve our purposes (however good those

1. J.R.R. Tolkien, "On Fairy-stories," in *Tolkien On Fairy-stories*, ed. Verlyn Flieger and Douglas A. Anderson (London: HarperCollins, 2014), 66.

purposes may be), we will find that it breaks in our hands. In contrast, when we draw upon works of literature that are beautiful and intriguing in their own right, in a spirit of genuine appreciation, we can confidently invite others to join us in discussing these tales. There is no 'bait and switch,' only the confidence that these classic works of literature *also* lead us to reflect on the truths of the faith.

Here it is useful to consider C.S. Lewis's distinction between 'using' and 'receiving,' which appears in his important book *An Experiment in Criticism*. To *use* a work of art or literature is to consider it in terms of what we can get out of it. Lewis warns that many readers, even highly sophisticated ones, have the mistaken belief "that all good books are good primarily because they give us knowledge, teach us 'truths' about 'life.'" Such insights are valuable, to be sure, but in focusing the reading experience on the extraction of these "truths," the reader has not actually attended to the text at all, in itself – it becomes merely a sort of literary quarry for mining insights. In contrast, to *receive* a work of art is a kind of surrender: "Real appreciation demands the opposite process. . . . We must begin by laying aside as completely as we can all our own preconceptions, interests, and associations."[2]

As Lewis explains, every literary work has two elements: it is both *logos* and *poiema*, something said and something made. If we attend only to the *logos*, the message or theme of the text, we miss out on an essential aspect of the literary experience. Works of literature, Lewis says, are "complex and carefully made objects. Attention to the very objects they are is our first step. To value them chiefly for reflections which they may suggest to us or morals we may draw from them, is a flagrant instance of 'using' instead of 'receiving.'"[3]

It is indeed possible to rightly 'use' literature, approaching it with an eye toward the results of engagement rather than purely on the experience itself; indeed, that is the entire focus of this book. However, this approach must always be balanced by an element of engagement with the text in itself: we must also first 'receive' it as a story or poem. I say *must*, because if we approach literature as if it were *just* a tool by which we can teach people about Christianity, it will cease to be effective even for that use! Great stories and poems are like living things: their value to us is precisely in that they are vital and dynamic, not reducible to doctrinal points or pedagogic insights.

It is worth making a distinction, as well, between *appreciation* and *enjoyment*. To appreciate something is to recognize its value and merits; to enjoy something is to like it or find it personally satisfying. It's important to appreciate a wide

2. C.S. Lewis, *An Experiment in Criticism*, chap. 3.
3. C.S. Lewis, chap. 8.

range of literature – but we may not enjoy all of it! This is perfectly good and normal; we should not expect to like all that we encounter. Just because a work is considered a classic doesn't mean that you have to enjoy it! The texts that I've chosen come from a range of literary genres and forms, including myth, epic poetry, lyric poetry, and prose. Some of these forms will be more familiar to you or your students than others, some are easier to engage with than others, and some will be more interesting to you than others. It's not a moral or intellectual failing if you find that a classic text – or even an entire genre or time period of literature – just isn't to your taste. On the contrary, it's a healthy expression of individual differences in personality, and a recognition that the world of literature and the arts is vast and varied; there is something for everyone.

To be sure, we should *try* to like a variety of different forms, genres, and styles. Enjoyment isn't a 'once and for all' proposition. As with encountering a strongly flavored new food, if we give ourselves the opportunity to come to terms with it gradually, in small bites, we may well discover that there's something nicely flavorful about this new cuisine after all! But it may well be that even after a wholehearted attempt to like it, you just don't. I, for one, dislike mushrooms (it is very un-hobbit-like of me, I know!), and I don't personally enjoy reading Dante's *Divine Comedy*, despite the fact that I *appreciate* it as a work of great literature. We all have different tastes and preferences, and this is entirely to the good. Being able to appreciate works that we don't personally enjoy helps us to develop intellectual and aesthetic humility, and makes it possible to recommend useful resources for a wider range of people. When it comes to choosing what to focus on for our work in evangelization, discipleship, and catechesis, we can be aware that it makes for more effective engagement when we share and discuss the kinds of stories that we both appreciate and enjoy.

Cultivating intellectual hospitality

This receptive and appreciative approach will help us to develop *intellectual hospitality*, an essential quality if we are to evangelize with the aid of these great stories.

Intellectual hospitality means seeking *first* to understand and only *then* to critique as necessary. It's in short supply these days, sadly undermined by our media consumption and by the generally polarized nature of discourse today. Our modern culture is a hypercritical one: our first reaction to anything different tends to be fault-finding. We certainly see that in people attacking Christianity or the Church, and we also see it in the assumptions held often even by genuine seekers. "Isn't the Catholic Church anti-woman? If God is good, how can there be evil? Doesn't having faith mean rejecting science?" We do have good responses to these criticisms, *if* people are willing to listen. But it's very easy for an evangelist to end up always on the defensive. If we're only responding to objections, we never have the chance to make a positive case. We need to be able to turn the tables and show the *goodness* of Christianity.

Now, how do we create an environment of genuine intellectual hospitality, in which all participants are willing to consider new ideas, to understand a point of view before taking a position about it? For us as evangelists and teachers, a key part of this process is understanding *what it feels like* for someone to be confronted with a very strange, challenging, unsettling idea, whether it's a skeptic considering whether God exists at all, or a young Catholic facing up to the implications of the Incarnation. The Christian faith, properly presented, runs deeply contrary to what the world presents as the good life, and challenges us to die to ourselves. It's a natural reaction to draw back, or run away. An essential part of real evangelization and discipleship is helping people be brave enough to investigate new ideas.

We'll be able to do that with greater empathy and skill if we, too, have had the experience of grappling with new and challenging ways of experiencing the world – and our texts here give us plenty of opportunities to do so.

These texts invite the reader to enter into perspectives that are, in some cases, very different from our own; this experience is often both intellectually and emotionally challenging. In order to gain the most from our reading, we need to allow ourselves first to engage with it on its own terms and hold back from immediate reaction and judgment, whether that judgment is positive or negative. We can misunderstand or misappropriate a text by too-hasty, superficial agreement just as much as by knee-jerk disagreement.

In these works of literature, we will find many things that we have in common with our ancestors, but also many things that are different: assumptions about how the world works, views on what's important, attitudes about the way that human beings relate to each other and the world around them. Sometimes these different views hold important insights that will correct our modern errors; sometimes our modern perspective helps us to discern genuine errors of the past. We will also find that the aesthetic qualities of a piece – its literary beauty, its effectiveness as a story – do not always align with our assessment of it in moral or theological terms. If we resist the temptation to hasty summing-up, and take the time to fully exercise intellectual and imaginative hospitality, we'll find that the texts yield much more of value.

Two spiritual challenges

There are two particular challenges that we must face in our literary journey. The first of these is to resist a kind of spiritual pride in reading classic literature.

It is a serious mistake to think that the *new* is automatically more relevant and meaningful than the *old*. But it is equally a mistake to think that rejecting all that is new, and feeding our imaginations solely on the literature of the past, will bring us to spiritual or intellectual health. There is no merit in reading an old text simply because it's on a reading list, to be able to say, "I have read it." You will not be a better person simply from having read the *Odyssey* or the *Divine Comedy*; in fact, you might be morally worse off, if it encourages an attitude of intellectual pride or elitism. If we hide in the past, we'll never be able to engage with the present or be prepared for the future – just as if we focus only on the culture of the present, we lose the ability to gain a wider perspective and deeper wisdom. We need to be able to do both: engage with the culture of the past *and* engage with the culture of the present.[4]

Reading 'old books' can help us to grow in wisdom, but only if we approach this reading in the right spirit: with intellectual hospitality, patience, and humility. *Tales of Faith* is intended to be a guide and support in this endeavor, helping readers to cultivate a generous and discerning spirit as a reader.

The second challenge is to be patient.

All Christians are, through the grace of their baptism, part of the Mystical Body of Christ. As Catholics, we are physically united to Christ through the Eucharist, supported by the sacrament of Reconciliation (Confession), and in relationship with Mary and the entire communion of saints. We are all in this together! Nonetheless, spiritual growth is always personal and individual. No one can make someone else grow. We can support and nurture spiritual growth, providing opportunities for it and role models of it, but ultimately it always occurs organically, through the work of the Holy Spirit. It is like gardening: as St. Paul observes about the process of discipleship, "neither the one who plants nor the one who waters is anything, but only God who gives the growth" (1 Cor. 3:7).

How does this relate to evangelization and discipleship through literature? When we're enthusiastic about any approach to spiritual growth, it can be

4. That this widely chronological approach is fruitful can be seen in the example of J.R.R. Tolkien, a devout Catholic and the author of *The Lord of the Rings*. Tolkien was a supremely knowledgeable scholar of medieval literature, with a solid grounding in ancient literature as well – and he also read widely and deeply in modern literature. For more on this, see my *Tolkien's Modern Reading: Middle-earth Beyond the Middle Ages* (Word on Fire Academic, 2021).

very easy and tempting to think of it as a surefire program that just has to be implemented properly. Thus, we can fall into the trap of treating literature as something that *will* get the results we want, if we only choose the right texts, ask the right questions, and have the right activities.

Literature (and the arts broadly speaking) seldom produce 'results' in that way: predictable, quantifiable, on schedule. Therefore, it is often the case that, precisely because we care so deeply for the conversion and formation of others, we become impatient, frustrated, even angry. The consequent negative attitude can turn outward, blaming others ("They're just not getting it; they don't care"), or inward, blaming ourselves ("I'm a lousy teacher; I'm useless for evangelization").

This experience of frustration or disappointment is extremely common; in fact, you should expect to feel it at some point (if you don't, then give thanks to God for this blessing).

We are so thoroughly enmeshed in a results-oriented, fast-paced culture (within the Christian community as well as outside it) that we have nearly all assimilated certain unhealthy and unrealistic expectations about the speed and visibility of 'results' in whatever we do. But humans are not machines; this way of thinking is inherently antithetical to real relationships. One of the great blessings of using literature in evangelization and discipleship is precisely that stories and poems naturally resist being instrumentalized and quantified. To read great literature and reflect on it is, by the very nature of the activity, to step off the treadmill for at least a moment. It is an opening for the operation of grace, and one that we sorely need in our distracted, overly busy culture.

The essential insight here is that we must be *patient*. It takes time for a relationship with Christ to grow, and it takes time even for the conditions of that growth to be established! We must be patient as we provide time and opportunity for people both to let down their guard and to learn *how* to reflect on issues of faith. It can, in fact, be painful for people to slow down and begin to engage with these questions, because it is often the case that we use distraction and busyness as avoidance-behavior, as excuses not to face the things that trouble us or the questions that, if answered, might require us to change our lives. Evangelization and discipleship are always slow processes if we are doing them well.

We can greatly help people along in this process by providing modes of evangelization and discipleship that nourish both the intellect and the imagination, and by presenting opportunities for deep personal engagement without pressure. Literature and the arts find a valued place here, but in order to use them well, we need to appreciate the particular way that they are valuable.

Engagement with literature provides incremental, gradual, subtle growth; it creates connections that provide for later insights; it establishes meaning that enables further growth. Discussion and engagement with literature is a profoundly *quiet* and *hidden* type of formation: it nourishes the roots of the plants in the garden and allows for seeds to be planted and to grow, and to unfold into leaf and flower at some later time. Patience and prayer are essential!

Practical advice

In order to get the most out of this journey through great literature, I encourage all readers of this book to adopt the following three practices as you engage with the materials here or lead others through them:

1. Take time.

Don't rush through the readings and activities; linger over them. I recommend doing a relatively quick read-through of the book as a whole, to get a sense of the different texts and themes; then come back to the particular works that you find most interesting, for a more in-depth reading. When you are working with a group, take time to read aloud from the text, either the work as a whole (if it is short) or a passage from it. Ensuring that the group *hears* the text or relevant passage first, as a whole literary piece, helps guard against superficial responses. This additional time to *receive* the text, to appreciate it as a work of literature, is good in itself and will also enrich and support your *use* of it for evangelization and discipleship.

When you are leading an in-person discussion using these questions, allow time for participants to think about the questions before answering. Leave at least 10–15 seconds before you allow anyone to offer a response (this will feel like an eternity, so I recommend using the time to silently pray a Hail Mary, which is just about the right length.) Alternatively, give half a minute or a minute for everyone to write down a thought or two. In this way, you will encourage the habit of genuine reflection rather than instant reaction and also provide opportunities for the quieter or less extroverted participants to share their thoughts.

If one particular question proves fruitful, stay with it. Don't feel obliged to go on to other questions: follow the conversation where it goes, as long as it is constructive.

2. Cultivate the habit of attention.

Many people today have difficulty with reading complex texts of any kind, even when they want to do so, because our culture tends toward constant attentional fragmentation. We are constantly bombarded by distractions: the chimes of text messages, the beeps and pop-ups of social media notifications, the allure of the next suggested video, the next item on the newsfeed, or the next episode in the watch list. We are often also overscheduled and busy, rushing from one activity to the next; our attention may be further fragmented by anxiety and stress. The result is that it can be very difficult for people to stay focused on any one task for more than a few minutes. We have become so accustomed to the little adrenaline rush of switching our attention from one thing to the next that sustained attention sometimes feels, by comparison, boring. It can be distressing if you realize that your ability to focus is not what it used to be (or what it ought to be), or if you find that your students or children are having difficulty paying enough attention to benefit from these texts. Fortunately, we need not despair.

Attention is like a muscle that gains strength from use. A useful strategy to build up 'attention strength' is the following. As you begin your reading session, first remove *exterior* distractions: put away cell phones; close all those browser tabs; turn off push notifications for your media. If you are leading a group, have participants place their phones completely out of sight (in a backpack, covered by a notebook). If the phone is in sight, it provides a constant reminder that there could be notifications to attend to, subtly stoking anxiety and distraction. Having the device out of sight genuinely helps in cultivating focus. Then, provide a scaffolding device for sustaining *interior* attention to the text. Scaffolding comes in many forms. For silent reading, it could include annotating the text as you read, with thoughts and questions in the margins, or keeping a journal of responses during reading. For group activities, it could include a dynamic group read-aloud, switching readers often. Another type of attentional scaffolding involves combining some sort of physical activity with hearing the text: if one's body is physically engaged with some activity, it can help to reduce mental distraction. Perhaps you can read the text aloud as you take your group for a walk, provide rosaries for participants to handle while they listen and discuss, or have students draw while you read. Don't assume that things like fidgeting, doodling, or looking out the window are indications of inattention; quite the opposite! It may well be the way in which these individuals best focus their attention.

In *Tales of Faith*, the selections that I have provided are all relatively short, either as complete pieces or as excerpts. Mainly, this is because their purpose is to provide a taste of the work, so that you can decide whether or not you'll read more of it. But it's also because I am aware that many (perhaps most) readers will find it challenging to read these works at full length, and I wish to provide excerpts of a length that isn't intimidating. If your attention, or your students' attention, needs some building up, that's OK! Start with the shorter pieces and practice scaffolding. As you and your group experience the rewards of sustained attention, it will become easier to stretch to longer pieces.

3. Pray.

Prayer, the most basic and foundational of activities, is surprisingly easy to leave out when planning activities for engaging with literature. Be deliberate and intentional about including prayer in your reading of this book and all teaching or discussion-leading that you do with it. For instance, you might consider inviting the Holy Spirit to be present in and through your reading, reflection, activities, and discussion; pausing to offer up to God anything that you find moving, troubling, or significant as you read. Consider also finding a particular patron saint whose intercession you value as you work through these readings.

At the end of this book, in chapter 7, you will find prayers and reflections from the saints that I have found especially valuable for literary study. Godspeed your reading!

Chapter Three

ANCIENT LITERATURE

Backgrounds and Context: Myths and Legends

What is a myth? The word comes from the Greek *mythos*, meaning "speech, discourse, story." In literary terms, myth is not simply a false or discredited belief, although that's how it's often used in everyday language, where we hear about 'debunking' or 'busting' myths. Rather, a myth is a story that deals with the biggest questions of human existence and the most fundamental human experiences. In the broadest sense, myths are narratives that give meaning and order to our lives.

Taken as a whole, 'myth' understood in the literary sense has the following characteristics:

- It is imaginatively rich, such that the mythic story is productive of further storytelling, drama, art, philosophy, and religious reflection.
- It features characters whose actions resonate with fundamental human experiences (such as birth, death, sexuality, discovery of identity, journeying); the stories may also touch on big questions such as the creation of the earth and life after death.
- It can be attributed to no specific original author, though it may be retold by named authors.
- It is set in a non-historical past or 'once upon a time' and does not attempt to link to verifiable historical events.

Narratives such as the hero's journey, the descent to the underworld, quests for secret wisdom, or death and resurrection are potent myths, in this sense, because they are resonant with meaning that helps us understand what it means to be human. The meaning conveyed by these myths (or archetypes, as they are sometimes called in literary or psychological terms) is accessible to all readers regardless of whether they share the underlying religious or philosophical beliefs expressed in a particular myth. We need not be ancient Greek or Roman polytheists to find something deeply moving and resonant about Aeneas's descent into Hades, or Phaeton's ill-fated adventure.

The Christian story is *not* a 'myth' in the full sense of the term here: the first two points apply, but the second two do not. However, we can rightly say that Christianity is myth-like (or mythopoeic): it is a story that is profoundly meaningful and imaginatively resonant, addressing the deepest questions of human life. At the same time, while having these mythic qualities, Christianity is also historically and metaphysically true. (It is worth noting that the fourth point does *not* apply to the book of Genesis, regardless of what view one takes of the timescale or chronology involved. The mode of expression is poetic, but the creation account in Genesis is explicitly connected to, and in context with, historical events recounted later in Genesis and in the rest of Scripture. The scriptural account of creation is presented as part of history, which is entirely different from the creation accounts found in other myths.)

As C.S. Lewis put it, "The heart of Christianity is a myth which is also a fact. The old myth of the Dying God, *without ceasing to be a myth*, comes down from the heaven of legend and imagination to the earth of history. It *happens* – at a particular date, in a particular place, followed by definable historical consequences."[1] J.R.R. Tolkien makes the same point: "The Gospels contain a fairy-story, or a story of a larger kind which embraces all the essence of fairy-stories. . . . But this story has entered History and the primary world; the desire and aspiration of sub-creation has been raised to the fulfillment of Creation."[2] We know from the Gospels, the epistles, and Church history that Christ's life, death, and Resurrection are events that really happened; the fact that they also have mythic resonance comes from the fact that their author is God himself.

Recognizing this mythopoeic aspect of Christianity is fruitful for evangelization in two ways. First, it allows us to invite non-believers into imaginative engagement with Christian literature, without pressure to accept it as fact just yet; and second, it means that the actual pagan myths provide an entry point to engagement with what Lewis calls "the myth made fact."

1. C.S. Lewis, "Myth Became Fact," in *Essay Collection and Other Short Pieces* (London: HarperCollins, 2000), 141.

2. J.R.R. Tolkien, "On Fairy-stories," in *Tolkien On Fairy-stories*, ed. Verlyn Flieger and Douglas A. Anderson (London: HarperCollins, 2014), 77–78.

A *legend* is, in literary terms, a story that lacks direct supporting evidence but could or might be true, unlike a myth, which is set in a nonhistorical and thus unverifiable setting. The word comes from the Middle Latin *legenda*, "things to be read," from the Latin *legere*, "to read, to gather, to select." *Legenda* originally referred to stories about saints' lives that were important enough to be written down; only later did it become associated with stories that included the supernatural or the highly dramatic and heroic. In casual usage, 'legend' or 'legendary' is sometimes used to refer to anything particularly impressive, including real people (think of 'sports legends'!) and events that we know to have happened.

Many historical figures and events later had legends develop around them, but not all miraculous stories are legendary. For instance, St. Francis, the twelfth-century founder of the Franciscan order, is said to have convinced a starving wolf to live peacefully with the people of a rural village; this is probably a later legend. St. Francis also received the stigmata, experiencing in his own body the five wounds of Christ, after having a vision of the crucified Christ. The episode of the stigmata is not legendary: it is verified by contemporary accounts. More significantly, the miracles of Jesus, including his Resurrection, were written down within the lifetime of eyewitnesses, so that there was simply not enough time for development of legends.

The origins of myths are shrouded in time: all written versions are adaptations of older stories, often contradictory and fragmentary, that were preserved through oral tradition, visual art, and theater. This older material was retold and put into order later – sometimes by authors who are 'ancient' to us now, as with Ovid's retellings of Greek myths in the *Metamorphoses*, and sometimes much more recently, as with Elias Lönnrot's nineteenth-century compilation of the Finnish *Kalevala*. We should, therefore, always be aware that there are no 'original' or 'authentic' texts: all the authors, whether they were classical poets or modern scholars, necessarily had to make interpretations and extrapolations from fragmentary and conflicting evidence. Furthermore, the imaginatively potent quality of myths means that authors have continued to adapt, retell, and reshape these tales for new audiences and contexts.

For Christian readers, it is especially important to realize that there is not, for any collection of mythology, a coherent, authoritative version of the myths: there is no 'pagan Bible.' Many of the apparent parallels between myths and the life of Jesus, which are sometimes claimed to debunk the Gospels, are the result of modern-day selection and adaptation. To be sure, we do find intriguing echoes, as with the 'dying and rising' themes to be found in myths such as those featuring the Greek Dionysius, the Egyptian Osiris, or the Norse Balder. But three points should be emphasized.

First, many arguments for 'pagan sources' for the Resurrection compile material from multiple sources, selecting the most notable details from each (and omitting material that doesn't fit) to form a composite picture that looks like a version of the Christian story. When we do compare 'apples to apples' and look at the pagan parallels in context, not slicing and reassembling them with an agenda in mind, the connections are typically much less striking. The connections are there, but as intriguing fragments and hints, not as exact detailed correspondences.

Second, the divine inspiration of the Bible worked through human authors; the Scriptures, both the Old and New Testaments, are written in the literary forms and styles of each human author's own time. No writer works in a vacuum; the human writers of Scripture would have known the literature of their day and necessarily have been influenced by it. If a scriptural author chose to use a literary form, a turn of phrase, or a striking image from a pagan source, this in no way affects or detracts from the divine inspiration of the work – no more than the human author using a particular language and writing system. Christians, then, need not be anxious about noticing possible parallels or literary influences in the myths that they read. The Bible's inspiration did not require the authors to live in a sort of literary isolation chamber.

Third, insofar as we do see echoes of Jesus in ancient myths, it is in fact an argument that *supports* the claims of Christianity. Because the Incarnation, Crucifixion, and Resurrection of our Lord are cosmic events, and furthermore are cosmic events that God knew from the beginning would take place, we should expect there to be echoes from those events going both forward and backward in time. We humans tend to forget that although we are time-bound, living only in one temporal direction, God is not bound in the same way; time is something he created, like space and matter.

In *Tales of Faith*, rather than choosing a selection of myths from a variety of sources, I have focused on selections only from the myths of the ancient Greeks. This was a difficult decision, as there are so many great treasure troves of myth, including the Mesopotamian *Gilgamesh*; Native American stories of Coyote; the Norse adventures of Odin, Thor, Loki, and Balder; tales of dragons in Chinese myth; and many more. My aim here is to encourage a deep engagement with a particular body of tales, allowing the reader to get a sense of the flavor of the stories and the texture of this mythological world, and to get a sense of how myths function. I encourage readers to move further and explore other mythologies as well.

The Greek Myths

These imaginatively powerful tales have provided rich material for generations of authors, artists, sculptors, painters, and filmmakers, and they continue to do so today. Some are tales of great beauty, such as the story of Cupid and Psyche; some are horrific, such as Chronos devouring his children; and some are tragic, such as Orpheus and Eurydice. There are vivid characters as well: some are admirable, like Athena, goddess of wisdom and war; others are all-too-familiar in their flaws, like the lecherous and power-abusing Zeus or the greedy King Midas; others are tragic, like Echo, who yearns for the self-absorbed Narcissus.

Here we can see a reply to the modern atheist claim: that since Christians don't believe in gods like Zeus and Athena, we're really atheists too: self-identified atheists just disbelieve in one more god than we do. What Christians mean by 'God' is not even remotely the same as the 'gods' in the classic myths. The Greek gods and goddesses are not all-powerful or all-wise, and certainly none are all-good. Most importantly, they are *beings*: powerful ones, but still creatures, not the Creator. We are talking about completely different things.

There is a mismatch or disconnect between the gods of the Greek myths and the awareness of the transcendent Creator that the Greek people (like all people) could discern through nature and their own conscience. And so there's a certain fortunate inconsistency in the way the Greek poets and philosophers talk about the gods. Zeus in particular is often referred to in contradictory ways: on the one hand, he's the rather unpleasant character in the stories, and on the other hand, he's the father-figure, the one who brings justice – the true king, not just the powerful tyrant. In fact, the ancient Greek view of 'Zeus' changed over time as their philosophy developed.

When we look at the Greek myths, we should keep in mind that they are not static, but part of an ongoing development of culture, philosophy, and art, which I would suggest is part of God's preparation of the pagan peoples to receive the light of Christ. There are many questions that the pagan view of the gods, as they appear in the stories, doesn't answer. If the gods are unpredictable, how can we understand the world at all? How was the world created? If the gods are not good, why do we have a sense of morality? The Greek philosophers began to move toward a form of ethical monotheism, belief in one God, an eternal spirit, what the philosopher Plato would call the Form of the Good. They sometimes used the term 'Zeus' to refer to this God, but increasingly, what they meant by it is not the same 'kind' of god as Zeus the character in the older myths. It is this more philosophical idea of Zeus that St. Paul is repurposing when he quotes a pagan poet as saying "we too are his offspring" (Acts 17:28).

By the time that the Greek gods are absorbed into the Roman pantheon and given Roman names, Zeus – now identified as Jupiter or Jove – has little to do with the philandering character of the early myths.

In late antiquity and medieval culture, Jupiter becomes an image of the kingliness of our Creator God, associated with festivity, justice, and royalty. It's *this* image of Jupiter that's taken up in the medieval associations of kingliness with the planet Jupiter. Indeed, we see in medieval Christian literature what we might call a 'baptizing' or at any rate an appropriation of the Greek and Roman pantheon. The gods, in their association with the seven 'planets' of the medieval cosmos, became what C.S. Lewis called "spiritual symbols" that have "permanent value"; Lewis himself would eventually make use of them in his Chronicles of Narnia. As Michael Ward explains, "Lewis had a high view of archetypes in general . . . and he was interested, in particular, in the literary use of 'archetypal patterns.' Giants, dragons, paradises, gods, and the like are 'the expression of certain basic elements in man's spiritual experience.' Such symbols, in Lewis's view, were able to reach a broader audience and touch deeper parts of an audience than realistic novels because they spring from a more fundamental source."[3]

The Greek pantheon

Note: Nearly all the classical gods and goddesses have both a Greek and a Roman name, and there are variants in the spelling of these names. I generally use the Greek names, as these are more widely known, but I will note both names (if they differ) in the descriptions that follow for the major characters of the pantheon.

The ***Olympians*** are the major figures in the Greek pantheon, so named because they dwell on Mt. Olympus: they comprise Zeus, Poseidon, and Hades, who have divided up the rule of the world amongst themselves, along with Hera, Hestia, Ares, Athena, Hermes, Apollo, Artemis, Aphrodite, and Hephaestus. Let's consider each in turn.

---

3. C.S. Lewis, "The Alliterative Metre," in *Selected Literary Essays*, ed. Walter Hooper (New York: HarperOne, 2013), 23; Michael Ward, *Planet Narnia: The Seven Heavens in the Imagination of C.S. Lewis* (Oxford: Oxford University Press, 2008), 230.

Zeus (Roman name: Jupiter; also Jove) is the ruler of the land and of the Olympians; he is the wielder of great power, but is never considered omnipotent. His weapon of choice is the lightning bolt, and he is associated with the eagle. Zeus is married to Hera, but he is a serial adulterer and rapist, siring many children with mortal women.

Poseidon (Neptune) is one of Zeus's brothers and ruler of the seas. He is typically shown with a trident and rides in a chariot drawn by seahorses. We will see in the *Odyssey* how much trouble he causes for Odysseus.

Hades (Pluto) is also Zeus's brother and ruler of the underworld. As king of the dead, his name became associated with the idea of a shadowy afterlife. Since it is from below ground that gold and other precious metals and gems come, Hades is also the god of wealth, and it is from this that we get the word *plutocracy* for rule by the wealthy. In the myths, Hades is feared, but not hated; he is unpitying, but not evil. He does, however, kidnap Persephone (Prosperpine) to force her to be his wife.

Hera (Juno) is the wife of Zeus and is known as the protector of married women. She is extremely vengeful and vindictive in the myths, which is not terribly surprising given Zeus's behavior but is distinctly unfortunate for those mortal women who are the recipients of unwanted attention from her husband.

Hestia (Vesta) is one of Zeus's sisters, the virgin goddess of hearth and home. She was honored in Greek and Roman cities, but in the myths, she is more of a concept than a character with a personality.

Ares (Mars) is the god of war, the son of Zeus and Hera. He has an ongoing adulterous affair with Aphrodite, who is married to Hephaestus. Interestingly, Ares is also associated with vegetation.

Athena (Minerva) is the virgin goddess of wisdom and war; she sprang from her father Zeus's forehead. She's one of the few Olympians who behaves, on the whole, in a reasonably moral manner. She is also patron of the city of Athens. She is particularly associated with the owl.

Hermes (Mercury) is the trickster of the Olympians: he is a master thief and the patron of commerce, and is also the guide of the dead. He is notable for his winged shoes, and also for his caduceus: a staff with twin entwined snakes. Here we find an interesting echo of Moses's lifting up of the bronze serpent in Exodus.

Apollo (Helios) is the god of the sun and also of music, healing, and prophecy: the famous Oracle at Delphi was part of his cult. He is also associated with snakes.

Artemis (Diana) is the twin sister of Apollo; she is the goddess of hunting, of wild animals, and of virginity.

Aphrodite (Venus) is sometimes said to be a daughter of Zeus and other times to have been born out of sea-foam. She is known as the goddess of love, but it would probably be more accurate to call her the goddess of lust. She is married to Hephaestus, but unfaithful.

Hephaestus (Vulcan) is the son of Zeus and Hera. He was born crippled and weak, and in displeasure Hera threw him down from Mt. Olympus. He was rescued and raised by sea goddesses and became the blacksmith of the gods. He is associated with fire (hence the words 'vulcanism' and 'volcano') and, along with Athena, is the patron of handicrafts and a supporter of civilization. He is married to Aphrodite and is constantly dismayed by her adultery with Ares.

As you can see, the pantheon is quite a rogues' gallery! The deities and demigods of these tales are human beings writ large, displaying all the failings of ordinary men and women, but with extra power and scope for action and no moral code restraining them. The result is that the stories hold up a mirror to fallen human nature – and they also show us the way that the human experience itself provides glimpses of something greater.

SELECTION

"Juno and Io"

From *The Age of Fable* by Thomas Bulfinch

Juno one day perceived it suddenly grow dark, and immediately suspected that her husband had raised a cloud to hide some of his doings that would not bear the light. She brushed away the cloud, and saw her husband on the banks of a glassy river, with a beautiful heifer standing near him. Juno suspected the heifer's form concealed some fair nymph of mortal mould – as was, indeed the case; for it was Io, the daughter of the river god Inachus, whom Jupiter had been flirting with, and, when he became aware of the approach of his wife, had changed into that form.

Juno joined her husband, and noticing the heifer praised its beauty, and asked whose it was, and of what herd. Jupiter, to stop questions, replied that it was a fresh creation from the earth. Juno asked to have it as a gift. What could Jupiter do? He was loath to give his mistress to his wife; yet how refuse so trifling a present as a simple heifer? He could not, without exciting suspicion; so he consented. The goddess was not yet relieved of her suspicions; so she delivered the heifer to Argus, to be strictly watched.

Now Argus had a hundred eyes in his head, and never went to sleep with more than two at a time, so that he kept watch of Io constantly. He suffered her to feed through the day, and at night tied her up with a vile rope round her neck. She would have stretched out her arms to implore freedom of Argus, but she had no arms to stretch out, and her voice was a bellow that frightened even herself. She saw her father and her sisters, went near them, and suffered them to pat her back, and heard them admire her beauty. Her father reached her a tuft of grass, and she licked the outstretched hand. She longed to make herself known to him, and would have uttered her wish; but, alas! words were wanting. At length she bethought herself of writing, and inscribed her name – it was a short one – with her hoof on the sand. Inachus recognized it, and discovering that his daughter, whom he had long sought in vain, was hidden under this disguise, mourned over her, and, embracing her white neck, exclaimed, "Alas! my daughter, it would have been a less grief to have lost you altogether!" While he thus lamented, Argus, observing, came and drove her away, and took his seat on a high bank, from whence he could see all around in every direction.

Jupiter was troubled at beholding the sufferings of his mistress, and calling Mercury told him to go and despatch Argus. Mercury made haste, put his winged slippers on his feet, and cap on his head, took his sleep-producing wand, and leaped down from the heavenly towers to the earth. There he laid aside his wings, and kept only his wand, with which he presented himself as a shepherd driving his flock. As he strolled on he blew upon his pipes. These were what are called the Syrinx or Pandean pipes. Argus listened with delight, for he had never seen the instrument before. "Young man," said he, "come and take a seat by me on this stone. There is no better place for your flocks to graze in than hereabouts, and here is a pleasant shade such as shepherds love." Mercury sat down, talked, and told stories till it grew late, and played upon his pipes his most soothing strains, hoping to lull the watchful eyes to sleep, but all in vain; for Argus still contrived to keep some of his eyes open though he shut the rest.

Among other stories, Mercury told him how the instrument on which he played was invented. "There was a certain nymph, whose name was Syrinx, who was much beloved by the satyrs and spirits of the wood; but she would have none of them, but was a faithful worshipper of Diana, and followed the chase. You would have thought it was Diana herself, had you seen her in her hunting dress, only that her bow was of horn and Diana's of silver. One day, as she was returning from the chase, Pan met her, told her just this, and added more of the same sort. She ran away, without stopping to hear his compliments, and he pursued till she came to the bank of the river, where he overtook her, and she had only time to call for help on her friends the water nymphs. They heard and consented. Pan threw his arms around what he supposed to be the form of the nymph, and found he embraced only a tuft of reeds! As he breathed a sigh, the air sounded through the reeds, and produced a plaintive melody. The god, charmed with the novelty and with the sweetness of the music, said, 'Thus, then, at least, you shall be mine.' And he took some of the reeds, and placing them together, of unequal lengths, side by side, made an instrument which he called Syrinx, in honor of the nymph." Before Mercury had finished his story he saw Argus's eyes all asleep. As his head nodded forward on his breast, Mercury with one stroke cut his neck through, and tumbled his head down the rocks. O hapless Argus! the light of your hundred eyes is quenched at once! Juno took them and put them as ornaments on the tail of her peacock, where they remain to this day.

But the vengeance of Juno was not yet satiated. She sent a gadfly to torment Io, who fled over the whole world from its pursuit. She swam through the Ionian sea, which derived its name from her, then roamed over the plains of Illyria, ascended Mount Haemus, and crossed the Thracian strait, thence named the Bosphorus (cow-ford), rambled on through Scythia, and the country of the Cimmerians, and arrived at last on the banks of the Nile. At length Jupiter interceded for her, and upon his promising not to pay her any more attentions Juno consented to restore her to her form. It was curious to see her gradually recover her former self. The coarse hairs fell from her body, her horns shrank up, her eyes grew narrower, her mouth shorter; hands and fingers came instead of hoofs to her forefeet; in fine there was nothing left of the heifer, except her beauty. At first she was afraid to speak, for fear she should low, but gradually she recovered her confidence and was restored to her father and sisters.

SELECTION

"Midas and the Golden Touch"

From *A Book of Myths* by Jean Lang

Once upon a time the kingdom of Phrygia lacked a king, and in much perplexity, the people sought help from an oracle. The answer was very definite:

"The first man who enters your city riding in a car shall be your king."

That day there came slowly jogging into the city in their heavy, wooden-wheeled wain, the peasant Gordias and his wife and son, whose destination was the marketplace, and whose business was to sell the produce of their little farm and vineyard – fowls, a goat or two, and a couple of skinsful of strong, purple-red wine. An eager crowd awaited their entry, and a loud shout of welcome greeted them. And their eyes grew round and their mouths fell open in amaze when they were hailed as King and Queen and Prince of Phrygia.

The gods had indeed bestowed upon Gordias, the low-born peasant, a surprising gift, but he showed his gratitude by dedicating his wagon to the deity of the oracle and tying it up in its place with the wiliest knot that his simple wisdom knew, pulled as tight as his brawny arms and strong rough hands could pull. Nor could anyone untie the famous Gordian knot, and therefore become, as the oracle promised, lord of all Asia, until centuries had passed, and Alexander the Great came to Phrygia and sliced through the knot with his all-conquering sword.

In time Midas, the son of Gordias, came to inherit the throne and crown of Phrygia. Like many another not born and bred to the purple, his honours sat heavily upon him. From the day that his father's wain had entered the city amidst the acclamations of the people, he had learned the value of power, and therefore, from his boyhood onward, power, always more power, was what he coveted. Also his peasant father had taught him that gold could buy power, and so Midas ever longed for more gold, that could buy him a place in the world that no descendant of a long race of kings should be able to contest. And from Olympus the gods looked down and smiled, and vowed that Midas should have the chance of realising his heart's desire.

Therefore one day when he and his court were sitting in the solemn state that Midas required, there rode into their midst, tipsily swaying on the back of a gentle full-fed old grey ass, ivy-crowned, jovial and foolish, the satyr Silenus, guardian of the young god Bacchus.

With all the deference due to the friend of a god Midas treated this disreputable old pedagogue, and for ten days and nights on end he feasted him royally. On the eleventh day Bacchus came in search of his preceptor, and in deep gratitude bade Midas demand of him what he would, because he had done Silenus honour when to dishonour him lay in his power.

Not even for a moment did Midas ponder.

"I would have gold," he said hastily – "much gold. I would have that touch by which all common and valueless things become golden treasures."

And Bacchus, knowing that here spoke the son of peasants who many times had gone empty to bed after a day of toilful striving on the rocky uplands of Phrygia, looked a little sadly in the eager face of Midas, and answered: "Be it as thou wilt. Thine shall be the golden touch."

Then Bacchus and Silenus went away, a rout of singing revellers at their heels, and Midas quickly put to proof the words of Bacchus.

An olive tree grew near where he stood, and from it he picked a little twig decked with leaves of softest grey, and lo, it grew heavy as he held it, and glittered like a piece of his crown. He stooped to touch the green turf on which some fragrant violets grew, and turf grew into cloth of gold, and violets lost their fragrance and became hard, solid, golden things. He touched an apple whose cheek grew rosy in the sun, and at once it became like the golden fruit in the Garden of the Hesperides. The stone pillars of his palace as he brushed past them on entering, blazed like a sunset sky. The gods had not deceived him. Midas had the Golden Touch. Joyously he strode into the palace and commanded a feast to be prepared – a feast worthy of an occasion so magnificent.

But when Midas, with the healthy appetite of the peasant-born, would have eaten largely of the savoury food that his cooks prepared, he found that his teeth only touched roast kid to turn it into a slab of gold, that garlic lost its flavour and became gritty as he chewed, that rice turned into golden grains, and curdled milk became a dower fit for a princess, entirely unnegotiable for the digestion of man. Baffled and miserable, Midas seized his cup of wine, but the red wine had become one with the golden vessel that held it; nor could he quench his thirst, for even the limpid water from the fountain was melted gold when it touched his dry lips. Only for a very few days was Midas able to bear the affliction of his wealth. There was nothing now for him to live for. He could buy the whole earth if he pleased, but even children shrank in terror from his touch, and hungry and thirsty and sick at heart he wearily dragged along his weighty robes of gold. Gold was power, he knew well, yet of what worth was gold while he starved? Gold could not buy him life and health and happiness.

In despair, at length he cried to the god who had given him the gift that he hated.

"Save me, O Bacchus!" he said. "A witless one am I, and the folly of my desire has been my undoing. Take away from me the accursed Golden Touch, and faithfully and well shall I serve thee forever."

Then Bacchus, very pitiful for him, told Midas to go to Sardis, the chief city of his worshippers, and to trace to its source the river upon which it was built. And in that pool, when he found it, he was to plunge his head, and so he would, for evermore, be freed from the Golden Touch.

It was a long journey that Midas then took, and a weary and a starving man was he when at length he reached the spring where the river Pactolus had its source. He crawled forward, and timidly plunged in his head and shoulders. Almost he expected to feel the harsh grit of golden water, but instead there was the joy he had known as a peasant boy when he laved his face and drank at a cool spring when his day's toil was ended. And when he raised his face from the pool, he knew that his hateful power had passed from him, but under the water he saw grains of gold glittering in the sand, and from that time forth the river Pactolus was noted for its gold.

SELECTION

"Phaeton"

From *A Book of Myths* by Jean Lang

To Apollo, the sun-god, and Clymene, a beautiful ocean-nymph, there was born in the pleasant land of Greece a child to whom was given the name of Phaeton, the Bright and Shining One. The rays of the sun seemed to live in the curls of the fearless little lad, and when at noon other children would seek the cool shade of the cypress groves, Phaeton would hold his head aloft and gaze fearlessly up at the brazen sky from whence fierce heat beat down upon his golden head.

"Behold, my father drives his chariot across the heavens!" he proudly proclaimed. "In a little while I, also, will drive the four snow-white steeds."

His elders heard the childish boast with a smile, but when Epaphos, half-brother to Apollo, had listened to it many times and beheld the child, Phaeton, grow into an arrogant lad who held himself as though he were indeed one of the Immortals, anger grew in his heart. One day he turned upon Phaeton and spoke in fierce scorn:

"Dost say thou art son of a god? A shameless boaster and a liar art thou! Hast ever spoken to thy divine sire? Give us some proof of thy sonship! No more child of the glorious Apollo art thou than are the vermin his children, that the sun breeds in the dust at my feet."

For a moment, before the cruel taunt, the lad was stricken into silence, and then, his pride aflame, his young voice shaking with rage and with bitter shame, he cried aloud: "Thou, Epaphos, art the liar. I have but to ask my father, and thou shalt see me drive his golden chariot across the sky."

To his mother he hastened, to get balm for his hurt pride, as many a time he had got it for the little bodily wounds of childhood, and with bursting heart he poured forth his story.

"True it is," he said, "that my father has never deigned to speak to me. Yet I know, because thou hast told me so, that he is my sire. And now my word is pledged. Apollo must let me drive his steeds, else I am for evermore branded braggart and liar, and shamed amongst men."

Clymene listened with grief to his complaint. He was so young, so gallant, so foolish.

"Truly thou art the son of Apollo," she said, "and oh, son of my heart, thy beauty is his, and thy pride the pride of a son of the gods. Yet only partly a god art thou, and though thy proud courage would dare all things, it were mad folly to think of doing what a god alone can do."

But at last she said to him, "Naught that I can say is of any avail. Go, seek thy father, and ask him what thou wilt." Then she told him how he might find the place in the east where Apollo rested ere the labours of the day began, and with eager gladness Phaeton set out upon his journey. A long way he travelled, with never a stop, yet when the glittering dome and jewelled turrets and minarets of the Palace of the Sun came into view, he forgot his weariness and hastened up the steep ascent to the home of his father.

Phœbus Apollo, clad in purple that glowed like the radiance of a cloud in the sunset sky, sat upon his golden throne. The Day, the Month, and the Year stood by him, and beside them were the Hours. Spring was there, her head wreathed with flowers; Summer, crowned with ripened grain; Autumn, with his feet empurpled by the juice of the grapes; and Winter, with hair all white and stiff with hoar-frost. And when Phaeton walked up the golden steps that led to his father's throne, it seemed as though incarnate Youth had come to join the court of the god of the Sun, and that Youth was so beautiful a thing that it must surely live forever. Proudly did Apollo know him for his son, and when the boy looked in his eyes with the arrogant fearlessness of boyhood, the god greeted him kindly and asked him to tell him why he came, and what was his petition.

As to Clymene, so also to Apollo, Phaeton told his tale, and his father listened, half in pride and amusement, half in puzzled vexation. When the boy stopped, and then breathlessly, with shining eyes and flushed cheeks, ended up his story with: "And, O light of the boundless world, if I am indeed thy son, let it be as I have said, and for one day only let me drive thy chariot across the heavens!" Apollo shook his head and answered very gravely:

"In truth thou art my dear son," he said, "and by the dreadful Styx, the river of the dead, I swear that I will give thee any gift that thou dost name and that will give proof that thy father is the immortal Apollo. But never to thee nor to any other, be he mortal or immortal, shall I grant the boon of driving my chariot."

But the boy pled on:

"I am shamed for ever, my father," he said. "Surely thou wouldst not have son of thine proved liar and braggart?"

"Not even the gods themselves can do this thing," answered Apollo. "Nay, not even the almighty Zeus. None but I, Phœbus Apollo, may drive the flaming chariot of the sun, for the way is beset with dangers and none know it but I."

"Only tell me the way, my father!" cried Phaeton. "So soon I could learn."

Half in sadness, Apollo smiled.

"The first part of the way is uphill," he said. "So steep it is that only very slowly can my horses climb it. High in the heavens is the middle, so high that even I grow dizzy when I look down upon the earth and the sea. And the last piece of the way is a precipice that rushes so steeply downward that my hands can scarce check the mad rush of my galloping horses. And all the while, the heaven is spinning round, and the stars with it. By the horns of the Bull I have to drive, past the Archer whose bow is taut and ready to slay, close to where the Scorpion stretches out its arms and the great Crab's claws grope for a prey. . . ."

"I fear none of these things, oh my father!" cried Phaeton. "Grant that for one day only I drive thy white-maned steeds!"

Very pitifully Apollo looked at him, and for a little space he was silent.

"The little human hands," he said at length, "the little human frame! – and with them the soul of a god. The pity of it, my son. Dost not know that the boon that thou dost crave from me is Death?"

"Rather Death than Dishonour," said Phaeton, and proudly he added, "For once would I drive like the god, my father. I have no fear."

So was Apollo vanquished, and Phaeton gained his heart's desire.

From the courtyard of the Palace the four white horses were led, and they pawed the air and neighed aloud in the glory of their strength. They drew the chariot whose axle and pole and wheels were of gold, with spokes of silver, while inside were rows of diamonds and of chrysolites that gave dazzling reflection of the sun. Then Apollo anointed the face of Phaeton with a powerful essence that might keep him from being smitten by the flames, and upon his head he placed the rays of the sun. And then the stars went away, even to the Daystar that went last of all, and, at Apollo's signal, Aurora, the rosy-fingered, threw open the purple gates of the east, and Phaeton saw a path of pale rose-colour open before him.

With a cry of exultation, the boy leapt into the chariot and laid hold of the golden reins. Barely did he hear Apollo's parting words: "Hold fast the reins, and spare the whip. All thy strength will be wanted to hold the horses in. Go not too high nor too low. The middle course is safest and best. Follow, if thou canst, in the old tracks of my chariot wheels!" His glad voice of thanks for the godlike boon rang back to where Apollo stood and watched him vanishing into the dawn that still was soft in hue as the feathers on the breast of a dove.

Uphill at first the white steeds made their way, and the fire from their nostrils tinged with flame-colour the dark clouds that hung over the land and the sea. With rapture, Phaeton felt that truly he was the son of a god, and that at length he was enjoying his heritage. The day for which, through all his short life, he had longed, had come at last. He was driving the chariot whose progress even now was awaking the sleeping earth. The radiance from its wheels and from the rays he wore round his head was painting the clouds, and he laughed aloud in rapture as he saw, far down below, the sea and the rivers he had bathed in as a human boy, mirroring the green and rose and purple, and gold and silver, and fierce crimson, that he, Phaeton, was placing in the sky. The grey mist rolled from the mountain tops at his desire. The white fog rolled up from the valleys. All living things awoke; the flowers opened their petals; the grain grew golden; the fruit grew ripe. Could but Epaphos see him now! Surely he must see him, and realise that not Apollo but Phaeton was guiding the horses of his father, driving the chariot of the Sun.

Quicker and yet more quick grew the pace of the white-maned steeds. Soon they left the morning breezes behind, and very soon they knew that these were not the hands of the god, their master, that held the golden reins. Like an air-ship without its accustomed ballast, the chariot rolled unsteadily, and not only the boy's light weight but his light hold on their bridles made them grow mad with a lust for speed. The white foam flew from their mouths like the spume from the giant waves of a furious sea, and their pace was swift as that of a bolt that is cast by the arm of Zeus.

Yet Phaeton had no fear, and when they heard him shout in rapture, "Quicker still, brave ones! more swiftly still!" it made them speed onwards, madly, blindly, with the headlong rush of a storm. There was no hope for them to keep on the beaten track, and soon Phaeton had his rapture checked by the terrible realisation that they had strayed far out of the course and that his hands were not strong enough to guide them. Close to the Great Bear and the Little Bear they passed, and these were scorched with heat. The Serpent which, torpid, chilly and harmless, lies coiled round the North Pole, felt a warmth that made it grow fierce and harmful again. Downward, ever downward galloped the maddened horses, and soon Phaeton saw the sea as a shield of molten brass, and the earth so near that all things on it were visible. When they passed the Scorpion and only just missed destruction from its menacing fangs, fear entered into the boy's heart. His mother had spoken truth. He was only partly a god, and he was very, very young. In impotent horror he tugged at the reins to try to check the horses' descent, then, forgetful of Apollo's warning, he smote them angrily. But anger met anger, and the fury of the immortal steeds had scorn for the wrath of a mortal boy.

With a great toss of their mighty heads they had torn the guiding reins from his grasp, and as he stood, giddily swaying from side to side, Phaeton knew that the boon he had craved from his father must in truth be death for him.

And, lo, it was a hideous death, for with eyes that were like flames that burned his brain, the boy beheld the terrible havoc that his pride had wrought. That blazing chariot of the Sun made the clouds smoke, and dried up all the rivers and water-springs. Fire burst from the mountain tops, great cities were destroyed. The beauty of the earth was ravished, woods and meadows and all green and pleasant places were laid waste. The harvests perished, the flocks and they who had herded them lay dead. Over Libya the horses took him, and the desert of Libya remains a barren wilderness to this day, while those sturdy Ethiopians who survived are black even now as a consequence of that cruel heat. The Nile changed its course in order to escape, and nymphs and nereids in terror sought for the sanctuary of some watery place that had escaped destruction. The face of the burned and blackened earth, where the bodies of thousands of human beings lay charred to ashes, cracked and sent dismay to Pluto by the lurid light that penetrated even to his throne.

All this Phaeton saw, saw in impotent agony of soul. His boyish folly and pride had been great, but the excruciating anguish that made him shed tears of blood, was indeed a punishment even too heavy for an erring god.

From the havoc around her, the Earth at last looked up, and with blackened face and blinded eyes, and in a voice that was harsh and very, very weary, she called to Zeus to look down from Olympus and behold the ruin that had been wrought by the chariot of the Sun. And Zeus, the cloud-gatherer, looked down and beheld. And at the sight of that piteous devastation his brow grew dark, and terrible was his wrath against him who had held the reins of the chariot. Calling upon Apollo and all the other gods to witness him, he seized a lightning bolt, and for a moment the deathless Zeus and all the dwellers in Olympus looked on the fiery chariot in which stood the swaying, slight, lithe figure of a young lad, blinded with horror, shaken with agony. Then, from his hand, Zeus cast the bolt, and the chariot was dashed into fragments, and Phaeton, his golden hair ablaze, fell, like a bright shooting star, from the heavens above, into the river Eridanus. The steeds returned to their master, Apollo, and in rage and grief Apollo lashed them. Angrily, too, and very rebelliously did he speak of the punishment meted to his son by the ruler of the Immortals. Yet in truth the punishment was a merciful one. Phaeton was only half a god, and no human life were fit to live after the day of dire anguish that had been his.

Bitter was the mourning of Clymene over her beautiful only son, and so ceaselessly did his three sisters, the Heliades, weep for their brother, that the gods turned them into poplar trees that grew by the bank of the river, and, when still they wept, their tears turned into precious amber as they fell. Yet another mourned for Phaeton – Phaeton "dead ere his prime." Cycnus, King of Liguria, had dearly loved the gallant boy, and again and yet again he dived deep in the river and brought forth the charred fragments of what had once been the beautiful son of a god, and gave to them honourable burial. Yet he could not rest satisfied that he had won all that remained of his friend from the river's bed, and so he continued to haunt the stream, ever diving, ever searching, until the gods grew weary of his restless sorrow and changed him into a swan.

And still we see the swan sailing mournfully along, like a white-sailed barque that is bearing the body of a king to its rest, and ever and anon plunging deep into the water as though the search for the boy who would fain have been a god were never to come to an end.

To Phaeton the Italian Naiades reared a tomb, and inscribed on the stone these words:

Driver of Phœbus' chariot, Phaëton,
Struck by Jove's thunder, rests beneath this stone,
He could not rule his father's car of fire,
Yet was it much, so nobly to aspire.

RECOMMENDED RESOURCES

Thomas Bulfinch, *The Age of Fable*. First published in 1855, this volume remains a useful and readable version of the myths. It is often printed in an omnibus volume called *Bulfinch's Mythology*. Bulfinch includes many excerpts from poetry that draws on classical mythology, so that we see how later authors imaginatively appropriated the myths for their own purposes. This context, though limited to the nineteenth century, helps us recognize the myths as part of a living and dynamic literary tradition.

Stephen Fry, *Mythos Trilogy: The Greek Myths Reimagined* (comprising *Mythos*, *Heroes*, and *Troy*). These volumes feature the myths retold with considerable wit and flair by Fry, who is an actor and comedian as well as a writer.

Edith Hamilton, *Mythology: Timeless Tales of Gods and Heroes*. This volume is a classic, readable retelling of the Greek myths (with a few Norse myths added at the end for good measure).

Nathaniel Hawthorne, *A Wonder Book*. These are nineteenth-century retellings of a small selection of tales specifically for children. This is available free on Project Gutenberg, but the print edition from Yesterday's Classics, illustrated by Walter Crane, and the Pook Press edition, illustrated by Arthur Rackham, are especially worthwhile.

Robert Graves, *The Greek Myths*. This recommendation comes with a caveat. Graves' retellings of the myths are well done, but his commentary treats them as relating to a prehistoric religion of the Great Goddess, a theory that is not accepted by classical scholars. He also makes an idiosyncratic attempt to distinguish the 'true' version of the myths from what he considers false or inferior forms.

Louis Markos, *The Myth Made Fact: Reading Greek and Roman Mythology Through Christian Eyes*.

Michael Ward, *Planet Narnia: The Seven Heavens in the Imagination of C.S. Lewis* and *The Narnia Code* (a shorter distillation of *Planet Narnia*, with an emphasis on the Christian devotional aspect, suitable for younger readers).

QUESTIONS FOR DISCUSSION

1. What are the admirable qualities of the Greek gods and goddesses (or of some of them)? What are their negative qualities? What do these characters show us about fallen human nature?

2. How is Jesus's behavior in the Gospels different from the behavior of the gods in the Greek myths? Would any of his actions have surprised an ancient Greek person?

3. *Power* is a recurring theme in the Greek myths. Discuss.

4. The Greek myths are a product of a pre-Christian time and a culture that, furthermore, had no (or very little) contact with Judaism. How can we approach these stories with intellectual hospitality? What can we learn from them?

5. What qualities seem to be considered admirable in the Greek myths? Compare these to the Christian understanding of the virtues. Where are there shared values? Where are the Christian virtues different?

6. In what ways are the stories recounted in the Gospels similar to certain Greek myths? In what ways are they different? How do the Greek myths help us to see that God is *not* just a version of Zeus?

7. Identify some modern-day adaptations of the Greek myths (for instance, in superhero films and graphic novels). How are these different from, or similar to, the originals? What significance do you see in this?

USING THE ARTS

1. Locate artwork of scenes from Greek mythology. Share and discuss: What aspect of the myth is emphasized in different works? What do these artists add to our experience of the myths? Suggested examples include: *Venus and Mars* and *The Birth of Venus* by Botticelli; *Bacchus* and *Self-Portrait as the Sick Bacchus* by Caravaggio; *The Fall of Phaeton* by Johann Liss.

2. Find examples of the Greek gods used in popular culture: films, games, toys, comics, and advertising. How do these representations differ from the original stories? What aspects of the stories seem to capture the twenty-first-century imagination?

3. Have students reimagine a Greek myth in the modern day (for instance, King Midas as a CEO), writing and acting out a short dramatic skit. Discuss.

The *Odyssey*

The *Odyssey*, one of the greatest poems of ancient Greece, dates from around 700 or 800 BC. Its origins and even its author are shrouded in mystery. Both the *Iliad* and the *Odyssey* are attributed to Homer, who is traditionally said to have been a blind poet, but we know nothing except the name. It is probable that Homer composed these works as part of the oral tradition of Greek poetry, possibly as early as 1000 BC, and they were written down by a later poet.

Keeping in mind the *Odyssey*'s origin as a poem composed to be heard, not to be read silently, can help us engage with the poem now. Reading aloud, or hearing something read aloud, is a very different experience than reading silently, and it brings out different aspects of the text.

Along with the *Iliad*, the *Odyssey* deals with the events and aftermath of the Trojan War. Troy itself did exist – the ruins of the city were discovered by archaeologists in the nineteenth century – but the heroes and dramatic events associated with the Trojan War are the stuff of legend.

In the legend of the Trojan War, the trouble starts when Paris, prince of Troy, runs away with Helen, the most beautiful woman in the world, who is also the wife of Menelaus, king of Sparta. (The infatuation of Paris and Helen had its origins in meddling by the goddess Aphrodite.) Menelaus and a whole host of other Greek heroes, including Agamemnon, Achilles, and Odysseus, lay siege to Troy for ten years; they eventually defeat the Trojans and sack the city. Homer's *Iliad* takes place during the last year of the war itself, while the *Odyssey* centers on Odysseus's ten-year attempt to get home to Ithaca, an endeavor made much more difficult because he has offended the god Poseidon.

Although he is a warrior, Odysseus (whose Roman name is Ulysses) primarily succeeds because of his cleverness. He's able to get the job done – no matter whether his methods are strictly moral or not. This trickster quality to Odysseus makes him an interesting figure to consider as the 'hero' of the tale. Is he, in fact, a hero by our standards?

The episode with Polyphemus, the cyclops, is particularly useful to consider in this regard. Odysseus and his men are captured by Polyphemus, a giant, monstrous figure who traps them in a cave and proceeds to treat them as a living larder.

Polyphemus is an archetypal outsider. He is not just a giant, but a cyclops, his single eye making him human-like, yet not human. He's a shepherd, moving his flocks from one place to the next, so he is neither a farmer tied to the land nor a city dweller. He lives in a cave, not a proper house, and the other cyclopes are isolated: there is no community or mutual help.

The encounter of Odysseus with Polyphemus unfolds in a way that is unsettling if we try to have sympathy either for either one character or the other.

To begin with, Polyphemus is no amiable giant: he takes Odysseus and his men captive and, gruesomely, uses them as a food supply. This would have been doubly horrible to the ancient Greek audience, for the cyclops is not only murderous, he is inhospitable.

Today, we take for granted things like safe roads and hotels, but in the ancient world, travelers could be, and often were, robbed and killed on the road, and they had to rely on asking for hospitality at homes along the way. The coming of Christianity and the development of monastic life meant a major development in hospitality: indeed an important ministry of monasteries was to give shelter to travelers, where they could be assured of welcome and safety. But in Homer's time, the traveler would have relied on individual households to provide hospitality, and we do see numerous examples of good hospitality in the *Odyssey*.

Polyphemus, though, violates the norms of hospitality in a particularly horrible way. Not only does he imprison his guests, he eats them. In one sense, we can say that he doesn't *see* Odysseus and his men properly: he does not recognize them as beings worthy of respect, but rather as units of food who happen to be able to talk.

Odysseus eventually comes up with a plan for them to escape, but, rather unpleasantly, it involves deliberately allowing more of his men to be eaten. They get Polyphemus drunk, poke out his eye, and then slip past him among his sheep. The trickster quality of Odysseus is in view here as well. Because Odysseus has earlier given his name as "Noman," when Polyphemus cries out to his fellow cyclopes for assistance, they disregard him because he says that "No man has attacked me." Nevertheless, as they sail away, Odysseus cannot resist taunting Polyphemus and boastfully revealing his real name. Polyphemus calls on his father, the sea god Poseidon, to exact revenge – and Poseidon curses Odysseus with ten years of wandering.

Odysseus is clever, yes, but he is also ruthless and proud. Here we have a prototype of many anti-hero figures of modern culture, who are strangely compelling and attractive even while acting on impulses of anger, pride, and violence.

Yet there are also many glimmers of the good and admirable in the *Odyssey*. Odysseus is not a particularly moral character, but he displays bravery and resourcefulness. We see in Penelope, Odysseus's wife and Telemachus's mother, a woman who is intelligent, faithful, and resourceful. In Telemachus we see a young man who admires his father and wants to defend his mother Penelope from the horde of men who, presuming that Odysseus is dead, have overrun the household and are pressuring Penelope to marry one of them. Athena shows up disguised as the character Mentor and provides guidance and help in a way that we can definitely admire. It is a world that is alien, and yet familiar, and in that way, it can help us get a fresh perspective on our own culture.

SELECTION

Ulysses and the Cyclops Polyphemus

From Book IX of the *Odyssey*, translated by Samuel Butler

"I am Ulysses son of Laertes, reknowned among mankind for all manner of subtlety, so that my fame ascends to heaven. I live in Ithaca, where there is a high mountain called Neritum, covered with forests; and not far from it there is a group of islands very near to one another – Dulichium, Same, and the wooded island of Zacynthus. It lies squat on the horizon, all highest up in the sea towards the sunset, while the others lie away from it towards dawn. It is a rugged island, but it breeds brave men, and my eyes know none that they better love to look upon. The goddess Calypso kept me with her in her cave, and wanted me to marry her, as did also the cunning Aeaean goddess Circe; but they could neither of them persuade me, for there is nothing dearer to a man than his own country and his parents, and however splendid a home he may have in a foreign country, if it be far from father or mother, he does not care about it. Now, however, I will tell you of the many hazardous adventures which by Jove's will I met with on my return from Troy. . . .

"We sailed hence, always in much distress, till we came to the land of the lawless and inhuman Cyclopes. Now the Cyclopes neither plant nor plough, but trust in providence, and live on such wheat, barley, and grapes as grow wild without any kind of tillage, and their wild grapes yield them wine as the sun and the rain may grow them. They have no laws nor assemblies of the people, but live in caves on the tops of high mountains; each is lord and master in his family, and they take no account of their neighbours.

[Ulysses and his men land on a nearby island and consider the land of the Cyclopes; Ulysses then chooses a group to go with him to explore it.]

"When we got to the land, which was not far, there, on the face of a cliff near the sea, we saw a great cave overhung with laurels. It was a station for a great many sheep and goats, and outside there was a large yard, with a high wall round it made of stones built into the ground and of trees both pine and oak. This was the abode of a huge monster who was then away from home shepherding his flocks. He would have nothing to do with other people, but led the life of an outlaw. He was a horrid creature, not like a human being at all, but resembling rather some crag that stands out boldly against the sky on the top of a high mountain.

"I told my men to draw the ship ashore, and stay where they were, all but the twelve best among them, who were to go along with myself. I also took a goat-skin of sweet black wine which had been given me by Maron, son of Euanthes, who was priest of Apollo the patron god of Ismarus, and lived within the wooded precincts of the temple. When we were sacking the city we respected him, and spared his life, as also his wife and child; so he made me some presents of great value – seven talents of fine gold, and a bowl of silver, with twelve jars of sweet wine, unblended, and of the most exquisite flavour. Not a man nor maid in the house knew about it, but only himself, his wife, and one housekeeper: when he drank it he mixed twenty parts of water to one of wine, and yet the fragrance from the mixing-bowl was so exquisite that it was impossible to refrain from drinking. I filled a large skin with this wine, and took a wallet full of provisions with me, for my mind misgave me that I might have to deal with some savage who would be of great strength, and would respect neither right nor law.

"We soon reached his cave, but he was out shepherding, so we went inside and took stock of all that we could see. His cheese-racks were loaded with cheeses, and he had more lambs and kids than his pens could hold. They were kept in separate flocks; first there were the hoggets, then the oldest of the younger lambs and lastly the very young ones all kept apart from one another; as for his dairy, all the vessels, bowls, and milk pails into which he milked, were swimming with whey. When they saw all this, my men begged me to let them first steal some cheeses, and make off with them to the ship; they would then return, drive down the lambs and kids, put them on board and sail away with them. It would have been indeed better if we had done so but I would not listen to them, for I wanted to see the owner himself, in the hope that he might give me a present. When, however, we saw him my poor men found him ill to deal with.

"We lit a fire, offered some of the cheeses in sacrifice, ate others of them, and then sat waiting till the Cyclops should come in with his sheep. When he came, he brought in with him a huge load of dry firewood to light the fire for his supper, and this he flung with such a noise on to the floor of his cave that we hid ourselves for fear at the far end of the cavern. Meanwhile he drove all the ewes inside, as well as the she-goats that he was going to milk, leaving the males, both rams and he-goats, outside in the yards. Then he rolled a huge stone to the mouth of the cave – so huge that two and twenty strong four-wheeled waggons would not be enough to draw it from its place against the doorway. When he had so done he sat down and milked his ewes and goats, all in due course, and then let each of them have her own young. He curdled half the milk and set it aside in wicker strainers, but the other half he poured into bowls that he might drink it for his supper. When he had got through with all his work, he lit the fire, and then caught sight of us, whereon he said:

"'Strangers, who are you? Where do sail from? Are you traders, or do you sail the sea as rovers, with your hands against every man, and every man's hand against you?'

"We were frightened out of our senses by his loud voice and monstrous form, but I managed to say, 'We are Achaeans on our way home from Troy, but by the will of Jove, and stress of weather, we have been driven far out of our course. We are the people of Agamemnon, son of Atreus, who has won infinite renown throughout the whole world, by sacking so great a city and killing so many people. We therefore humbly pray you to show us some hospitality, and otherwise make us such presents as visitors may reasonably expect. May your excellency fear the wrath of heaven, for we are your suppliants, and Jove takes all respectable travellers under his protection, for he is the avenger of all suppliants and foreigners in distress.'

"To this he gave me but a pitiless answer, 'Stranger,' said he, 'you are a fool, or else you know nothing of this country. Talk to me, indeed, about fearing the gods or shunning their anger? We Cyclopes do not care about Jove or any of your blessed gods, for we are ever so much stronger than they. I shall not spare either yourself or your companions out of any regard for Jove, unless I am in the humour for doing so. And now tell me where you made your ship fast when you came on shore. Was it round the point, or is she lying straight off the land?'

"He said this to draw me out, but I was too cunning to be caught in that way, so I answered with a lie; 'Neptune,' said I, 'sent my ship on to the rocks at the far end of your country, and wrecked it. We were driven on to them from the open sea, but I and those who are with me escaped the jaws of death.'

"The cruel wretch vouchsafed me not one word of answer, but with a sudden clutch he gripped up two of my men at once and dashed them down upon the ground as though they had been puppies. Their brains were shed upon the ground, and the earth was wet with their blood. Then he tore them limb from limb and supped upon them. He gobbled them up like a lion in the wilderness, flesh, bones, marrow, and entrails, without leaving anything uneaten. As for us, we wept and lifted up our hands to heaven on seeing such a horrid sight, for we did not know what else to do; but when the Cyclops had filled his huge paunch, and had washed down his meal of human flesh with a drink of neat milk, he stretched himself full length upon the ground among his sheep, and went to sleep. I was at first inclined to seize my sword, draw it, and drive it into his vitals, but I reflected that if I did we should all certainly be lost, for we should never be able to shift the stone which the monster had put in front of the door. So we stayed sobbing and sighing where we were till morning came.

"When the child of morning, rosy-fingered Dawn, appeared, he again lit his fire, milked his goats and ewes, all quite rightly, and then let each have her own young one; as soon as he had got through with all his work, he clutched up two more of my men, and began eating them for his morning's meal. Presently, with the utmost ease, he rolled the stone away from the door and drove out his sheep, but he at once put it back again – as easily as though he were merely clapping the lid on to a quiver full of arrows. As soon as he had done so he shouted, and cried 'Shoo, shoo,' after his sheep to drive them on to the mountain; so I was left to scheme some way of taking my revenge and covering myself with glory.

"In the end I deemed it would be the best plan to do as follows. The Cyclops had a great club which was lying near one of the sheep pens; it was of green olive wood, and he had cut it intending to use it for a staff as soon as it should be dry. It was so huge that we could only compare it to the mast of a twenty-oared merchant vessel of large burden, and able to venture out into open sea. I went up to this club and cut off about six feet of it; I then gave this piece to the men and told them to fine it evenly off at one end, which they proceeded to do, and lastly I brought it to a point myself, charring the end in the fire to make it harder. When I had done this I hid it under dung, which was lying about all over the cave, and told the men to cast lots which of them should venture along with myself to lift it and bore it into the monster's eye while he was asleep. The lot fell upon the very four whom I should have chosen, and I myself made five. In the evening the wretch came back from shepherding, and drove his flocks into the cave – this time driving them all inside, and not leaving any in the yards; I suppose some fancy must have taken him, or a god must have prompted him to do so. As soon as he had put the stone back to its place against the door, he sat down, milked his ewes and his goats all quite rightly, and then let each have her own young one; when he had got through with all this work, he gripped up two more of my men, and made his supper off them. So I went up to him with an ivy-wood bowl of black wine in my hands:

"'Look here, Cyclops,' said I, you have been eating a great deal of man's flesh, so take this and drink some wine, that you may see what kind of liquor we had on board my ship. I was bringing it to you as a drink-offering, in the hope that you would take compassion upon me and further me on my way home, whereas all you do is to go on ramping and raving most intolerably. You ought to be ashamed yourself; how can you expect people to come see you any more if you treat them in this way?'

"He then took the cup and drank. He was so delighted with the taste of the wine that he begged me for another bowl full. 'Be so kind,' he said, 'as to give me some more, and tell me your name at once. I want to make you a present that you will be glad to have. We have wine even in this country, for our soil grows grapes and the sun ripens them, but this drinks like nectar and ambrosia all in one.'

"I then gave him some more; three times did I fill the bowl for him, and three times did he drain it without thought or heed; then, when I saw that the wine had got into his head, I said to him as plausibly as I could: 'Cyclops, you ask my name and I will tell it you; give me, therefore, the present you promised me; my name is Noman; this is what my father and mother and my friends have always called me.'

"But the cruel wretch said, 'Then I will eat all Noman's comrades before Noman himself, and will keep Noman for the last. This is the present that I will make him.'

"As he spoke he reeled, and fell sprawling face upwards on the ground. His great neck hung heavily backwards and a deep sleep took hold upon him. Presently he turned sick, and threw up both wine and the gobbets of human flesh on which he had been gorging, for he was very drunk. Then I thrust the beam of wood far into the embers to heat it, and encouraged my men lest any of them should turn faint-hearted. When the wood, green though it was, was about to blaze, I drew it out of the fire glowing with heat, and my men gathered round me, for heaven had filled their hearts with courage. We drove the sharp end of the beam into the monster's eye, and bearing upon it with all my weight I kept turning it round and round as though I were boring a hole in a ship's plank with an auger, which two men with a wheel and strap can keep on turning as long as they choose. Even thus did we bore the red hot beam into his eye, till the boiling blood bubbled all over it as we worked it round and round, so that the steam from the burning eyeball scalded his eyelids and eyebrows, and the roots of the eye sputtered in the fire. As a blacksmith plunges an axe or hatchet into cold water to temper it – for it is this that gives strength to the iron – and it makes a great hiss as he does so, even thus did the Cyclops' eye hiss round the beam of olive wood, and his hideous yells made the cave ring again. We ran away in a fright, but he plucked the beam all besmirched with gore from his eye, and hurled it from him in a frenzy of rage and pain, shouting as he did so to the other Cyclopes who lived on the bleak headlands near him; so they gathered from all quarters round his cave when they heard him crying, and asked what was the matter with him.

"'What ails you, Polyphemus,' said they, 'that you make such a noise, breaking the stillness of the night, and preventing us from being able to sleep? Surely no man is carrying off your sheep? Surely no man is trying to kill you either by fraud or by force?'

"But Polyphemus shouted to them from inside the cave, 'Noman is killing me by fraud! Noman is killing me by force!'

"'Then,' said they, 'if no man is attacking you, you must be ill; when Jove makes people ill, there is no help for it, and you had better pray to your father Neptune.'

"Then they went away, and I laughed inwardly at the success of my clever stratagem, but the Cyclops, groaning and in an agony of pain, felt about with his hands till he found the stone and took it from the door; then he sat in the doorway and stretched his hands in front of it to catch anyone going out with the sheep, for he thought I might be foolish enough to attempt this.

"As for myself I kept on puzzling to think how I could best save my own life and those of my companions; I schemed and schemed, as one who knows that his life depends upon it, for the danger was very great. In the end I deemed that this plan would be the best. The male sheep were well grown, and carried a heavy black fleece, so I bound them noiselessly in threes together, with some of the withies on which the wicked monster used to sleep. There was to be a man under the middle sheep, and the two on either side were to cover him, so that there were three sheep to each man. As for myself there was a ram finer than any of the others, so I caught hold of him by the back, esconced myself in the thick wool under his belly, and flung on patiently to his fleece, face upwards, keeping a firm hold on it all the time.

"Thus, then, did we wait in great fear of mind till morning came, but when the child of morning, rosy-fingered Dawn, appeared, the male sheep hurried out to feed, while the ewes remained bleating about the pens waiting to be milked, for their udders were full to bursting; but their master in spite of all his pain felt the backs of all the sheep as they stood upright, without being sharp enough to find out that the men were underneath their bellies. As the ram was going out, last of all, heavy with its fleece and with the weight of my crafty self; Polyphemus laid hold of it and said:

"'My good ram, what is it that makes you the last to leave my cave this morning? You are not wont to let the ewes go before you, but lead the mob with a run whether to flowery mead or bubbling fountain, and are the first to come home again at night; but now you lag last of all. Is it because you know your master has lost his eye, and are sorry because that wicked Noman and his horrid crew have got him down in his drink and blinded him? But I will have his life yet. If you could understand and talk, you would tell me where the wretch is hiding, and I would dash his brains upon the ground till they flew all over the cave. I should thus have some satisfaction for the harm this no-good Noman has done me.'

"As he spoke he drove the ram outside, but when we were a little way out from the cave and yards, I first got from under the ram's belly, and then freed my comrades; as for the sheep, which were very fat, by constantly heading them in the right direction we managed to drive them down to the ship. The crew rejoiced greatly at seeing those of us who had escaped death, but wept for the others whom the Cyclops had killed. However, I made signs to them by nodding and frowning that they were to hush their crying, and told them to get all the sheep on board at once and put out to sea; so they went aboard, took their places, and smote the grey sea with their oars. Then, when I had got as far out as my voice would reach, I began to jeer at the Cyclops.

"'Cyclops,' said I, 'you should have taken better measure of your man before eating up his comrades in your cave. You wretch, eat up your visitors in your own house? You might have known that your sin would find you out, and now Jove and the other gods have punished you.'

"He got more and more furious as he heard me, so he tore the top from off a high mountain, and flung it just in front of my ship so that it was within a little of hitting the end of the rudder. The sea quaked as the rock fell into it, and the wash of the wave it raised carried us back towards the mainland, and forced us towards the shore. But I snatched up a long pole and kept the ship off, making signs to my men by nodding my head, that they must row for their lives, whereon they laid out with a will. When we had got twice as far as we were before, I was for jeering at the Cyclops again, but the men begged and prayed of me to hold my tongue.

"'Do not,' they exclaimed, 'be mad enough to provoke this savage creature further; he has thrown one rock at us already which drove us back again to the mainland, and we made sure it had been the death of us; if he had then heard any further sound of voices he would have pounded our heads and our ship's timbers into a jelly with the rugged rocks he would have heaved at us, for he can throw them a long way.'

"But I would not listen to them, and shouted out to him in my rage, 'Cyclops, if any one asks you who it was that put your eye out and spoiled your beauty, say it was the valiant warrior Ulysses, son of Laertes, who lives in Ithaca.'

"On this he groaned, and cried out, 'Alas, alas, then the old prophecy about me is coming true. There was a prophet here, at one time, a man both brave and of great stature, Telemus son of Eurymus, who was an excellent seer, and did all the prophesying for the Cyclopes till he grew old; he told me that all this would happen to me some day, and said I should lose my sight by the hand of Ulysses. I have been all along expecting some one of imposing presence and superhuman strength, whereas he turns out to be a little insignificant weakling, who has managed to blind my eye by taking advantage of me in my drink; come here, then, Ulysses, that I may make you presents to show my hospitality, and urge Neptune to help you forward on your journey – for Neptune and I are father and son. He, if he so will, shall heal me, which no one else neither god nor man can do.'

"Then I said, 'I wish I could be as sure of killing you outright and sending you down to the house of Hades, as I am that it will take more than Neptune to cure that eye of yours.'

"On this he lifted up his hands to the firmament of heaven and prayed, saying, 'Hear me, great Neptune; if I am indeed your own true-begotten son, grant that Ulysses may never reach his home alive; or if he must get back to his friends at last, let him do so late and in sore plight after losing all his men."

"Thus did he pray, and Neptune heard his prayer. Then he picked up a rock much larger than the first, swung it aloft and hurled it with prodigious force. It fell just short of the ship, but was within a little of hitting the end of the rudder. The sea quaked as the rock fell into it, and the wash of the wave it raised drove us onwards on our way towards the shore of the island.

"When at last we got to the island where we had left the rest of our ships, we found our comrades lamenting us, and anxiously awaiting our return. We ran our vessel upon the sands and got out of her on to the sea shore; we also landed the Cyclops' sheep, and divided them equitably amongst us so that none might have reason to complain. As for the ram, my companions agreed that I should have it as an extra share; so I sacrificed it on the sea shore, and burned its thigh bones to Jove, who is the lord of all. But he heeded not my sacrifice, and only thought how he might destroy my ships and my comrades.

"Thus through the livelong day to the going down of the sun we feasted our fill on meat and drink, but when the sun went down and it came on dark, we camped upon the beach. When the child of morning, rosy-fingered Dawn, appeared, I bade my men on board and loose the hawsers. Then they took their places and smote the grey sea with their oars; so we sailed on with sorrow in our hearts, but glad to have escaped death though we had lost our comrades."

RECOMMENDED RESOURCES

There are many translations of the *Odyssey*, taking various approaches. The original Greek poem is difficult to render in English poetry, and some translators have made it into a prose narrative instead. Some verse translations aim to reproduce, as much as possible, the flavor and rhythm of the Greek original, while others take advantage of poetic devices (such as rhyme) that work well in English, even though these did not appear in the original, in order to create an experience that is as engaging for the English reader as the original is for the Greek reader.

Robert Fitzgerald, *The Odyssey* (modern verse translation).

Richmond Lattimore, *The Odyssey of Homer* (modern verse translation); this is my own personal favorite of the translations.

Alexander Pope, *The Odyssey* (eighteenth-century verse translation).

E.V. Rieu, *The Odyssey* (modern prose translation – Penguin Classics edition).

Gareth Hinds, *The Odyssey* (graphic novel).

C.S. Lewis, *A Preface to Paradise Lost.* This short book is indispensable for understanding the literary genre of the epic poem. Although focused on Milton's poem, the first chapters present an illuminating discussion of the genre of epic poetry. Chapters III, IV, and V, on "primary epic," are particularly valuable for an understanding of the *Odyssey.*

QUESTIONS FOR DISCUSSION

1. Is Odysseus a hero? What about Penelope? Why or why not? What do you consider to be the virtues a true hero should display? What virtues are celebrated or disregarded in modern films and stories about heroes?

2. What is the position of women in ancient Greek society, as depicted in the *Odyssey*? How does this differ from the Christian view of women?

3. How would the Beatitudes be received in the world of the *Odyssey*? Imagine the different reactions to Jesus's teaching of Odysseus, Penelope, Odysseus's sailors, and the slaves in Odysseus's household in Ithaca.

4. Consider Odysseus's method of escaping from Polyphemus. What do you think of his decision? Would you do the same? Why or why not?

5. Elsewhere in the *Odyssey*, we encounter the Sirens and also the island of the Lotus-Eaters. These scenes have been particularly striking to many later readers. What resonance do they have with what we know of the Christian life?

6. The conclusion of the *Odyssey* is extremely violent. Is Odysseus's treatment of the suitors an example of justice or of vengeance?

7. Christian tradition includes some pious legends that are unverified but may be true (for instance, the tradition that on the way to his Crucifixion, our Lord was comforted by St. Veronica, who wiped his face with a veil that then preserved his image). We also have some tales of the saints featuring miraculous events that probably did not happen. Yet we know that miracles do happen. How do we distinguish between historical fact, legend, myth, and simple falsehood in our teaching of children and our own devotional lives *without* also accidentally cultivating a materialist, skeptical attitude toward miracles and divine intervention?

8. The word 'odyssey' comes from this tale: from the name of its protagonist, Odysseus. This connection shows just how profoundly Homer's tale has entered into Western culture. What elements of the *structure* of the story are significant? In what way is the Christian journey an 'odyssey'?

USING THE ARTS

1. Locate images of artwork of scenes from the *Odyssey*. Print these out and shuffle them; add in cards that refer to any scenes for which you don't have an image. Have your group arrange the cards in a timeline. (You can be sneaky and add in an event that is *not* from the *Odyssey*, to see if they can identify that it doesn't fit in.) This activity encourages engagement with the storyline as a narrative and can lead to discussion about the relative importance of different events and their consequences.

2. Consider different representations in art of the Polyphemus episode (or others in the *Odyssey*). What aspects of the scene are highlighted or suggested in each piece of art? How do they differ? Have participants depict other scenes from the *Odyssey* in one of the styles of these works of art. Some options include: a Greek vase painting of Odysseus and Polyphemus; *Ulysses Fleeing the Cave of Polyphemus* by Christoffer Wilhelm Eckersberg; *Odysseus in the Cave of Polyphemus* by Constantin Hansen; *Ulysses Deriding Polyphemus* by J.M.W. Turner.

3. Write about your own experience of the Christian faith in the structure of the *Odyssey*. What would be the starting point? Is there a Mentor figure in this journey? What obstacles appeared on the journey, and how might they be imaginatively represented?

Oedipus Rex

Sophocles is one of the great Greek writers of tragedy, and *Oedipus Rex* (*Oedipus the King*) is his most famous work, composed around 400 BC. It dramatizes the rise and fall of the titular Oedipus and, in the process, vividly depicts the destructive power of pride.

In English, the word *pride* is complex. It does have positive meanings, such as a sense of satisfaction in something one has accomplished or achieved, or the admiration of others' achievements or merits. However, *pride* is primarily negative in its meaning. At its core, pride is self-centeredness: in the Christian tradition, it is listed as the first of the seven deadly sins for a good reason. Pride means to put oneself, not God, first. This kind of self-absorption can be seen in narcissism – which takes its name from the Greek myth of Echo and Narcissus, a tale that does not have a happy ending – as well as in snobbery, arrogance, overconfidence (often with disastrous results), and bullying. Pride is the original sin of Adam and Eve in the Garden of Eden, who were seduced into thinking that *they* knew better than God what they should and shouldn't do.

The ancient Greeks gave the name *hubris* to pride in the form of presumption and excessive self-confidence, usually linked with anger and violence. They recognized its destructive power, and indeed, it is often the fatal flaw that drives the action of Greek tragedy. In the Greek myths, we see a number of stories of *hubris* and the devastation it causes, as in King Midas, Icarus and Daedalus, and Phaeton.

In *Oedipus Rex*, Sophocles provides a complex and disturbing consideration of pride. To appreciate this, we need to do a brief overview of the story. Oedipus was the son of Laius and Jocasta of Thebes, but, due to a prophecy that he would murder his father, he was abandoned as an infant. Secretly handed over to the family of Polybius in Corinth, Oedipus grows up ignorant of his real parentage. Having heard for himself a prophecy that he would kill his father, he leaves Corinth and heads for Thebes, with the idea of thus preventing the prophecy from being fulfilled. On the way there, he kills Laius (while ignorant of his identity) in a pointless dispute over the right of way at a crossroads; eventually, he ends up marrying his now-widowed mother, Jocasta, and becoming king of Thebes.

It is in this context that the play *Oedipus Rex* begins. A plague has fallen upon Thebes, and the oracle of Apollo reveals that it is caused by an abomination in the city. Oedipus is told straightforwardly by the blind seer Tiresias that he, Oedipus, is the guilty one. However, disregarding and mocking Tiresias, Oedipus sets out to investigate and gradually pieces the puzzle together. Jocasta, having realized much sooner than Oedipus does that he is her son as well as her husband, begs him to leave off his questioning, but he insists. When he finds out the truth, Jocasta commits suicide, Oedipus blinds himself, and at his own request he is exiled from the city.

Could Oedipus have done anything to avert this gruesome situation? Or was he fated to commit murder and incest because of the prophecies? To a certain extent, he suffers through no fault of his own, as he did not know that Jocasta was his mother when he married her. However, Sophocles gives many indications that Oedipus's character flaw of *hubris* is, in fact, central to the disaster.

Oedipus acts hastily on what he understands as the interpretation of the prophecy he heard as a young man – without considering its ambiguity, seeking more information, or getting advice from anyone else. Although his motive is good – to avoid killing his (adoptive) father – his actions are based in overconfidence. He does not know that the man he kills at the crossroads is his (biological) father – but killing someone in a roadside brawl because he refuses to yield the right of way shows arrogance leading to deadly violence. And his later arrogance in disregarding Tiresias's warning means that when Oedipus eventually discovers the truth, it comes to him not in the context of sorrowful repentance, but as a catastrophe that shatters his world, precipitating the final, bloody course of events.

It's a grim and powerful depiction of the perils of pride.

SELECTION

"The Story of Oedipus"

A prose summary from *Old Greek Folk Stories Told Anew*
by Josephine Preston Peabody

Behind the power of the gods and beyond all the efforts of men, the three Fates sat at their spinning.

No one could tell whence these sisters were, but by some strange necessity they spun the web of human life and made destinies without knowing why. It was not for Clotho to decree whether the thread of a life should be stout or fragile, nor for Lachesis to choose the fashion of the web; and Atropos herself must sometimes have wept to cut a life short with her shears, and let it fall unfinished. But they were like spinners for some Power that said of life, as of a garment, *Thus it must be.* That Power neither gods nor men could withstand.

There was once a king named Laius (a grandson of Cadmus himself), who ruled over Thebes, with Jocasta his wife. To them an Oracle had foretold that if a son of theirs lived to grow up, he would one day kill his father and marry his own mother. The king and queen resolved to escape such a doom, even at terrible cost. Accordingly Laius gave his son, who was only a baby, to a certain herdsman, with instructions to put him to death.

This was not to be. The herdsman carried the child to a lonely mountain-side, but once there, his heart failed him. Hardly daring to disobey the king's command, yet shrinking from murder, he hung the little creature by his feet to the branches of a tree, and left him there to die.

But there chanced to come that way with his flocks, a man who served King Polybus of Corinth. He found the baby perishing in the tree, and, touched with pity, took him home to his master. The king and queen of Corinth were childless, and some power moved them to take this mysterious child as a gift. They called him Oedipus (Swollen-Foot) because of the wounds they had found upon him, and, knowing naught of his parentage, they reared him as their own son. So the years went by.

Now, when Oedipus had come to manhood, he went to consult the Oracle at Delphi, as all great people were wont, to learn what fortune had in store for him.

But for him the Oracle had only a sentence of doom. According to the Fates, he would live to kill his own father and wed his mother.

Filled with dismay, and resolved in his turn to conquer fate, Oedipus fled from Corinth; for he had never dreamed that his parents were other than Polybus and Merope the queen. Thinking to escape crime, he took the road towards Thebes, so hastening into the very arms of his evil destiny.

It happened that King Laius, with one attendant, was on his way to Delphi from the city Thebes. In a narrow road he met this strange young man, also driving in a chariot, and ordered him to quit the way. Oedipus, who had been reared to princely honors, refused to obey; and the king's charioteer, in great anger, killed one of the young man's horses. At this insult Oedipus fell upon master and servant; mad with rage, he slew them both, and went on his way, not knowing the half of what he had done. The first saying of the Oracle was fulfilled.

But the prince was to have his day of triumph before the doom. There was a certain wonderful creature called the Sphinx, which had been a terror to Thebes for many days. In form half woman and half lion, she crouched always by a precipice near the highway, and put the same mysterious question to every passer-by. None had ever been able to answer, and none had ever lived to warn men of the riddle; for the Sphinx fell upon every one as he failed, and hurled him down the abyss, to be dashed in pieces.

This way came Oedipus towards the city Thebes, and the Sphinx crouched, face to face with him, and spoke the riddle that none had been able to guess.

"*What animal is that which in the morning goes on four feet, at noon on two, and in the evening upon three?*"

Oedipus, hiding his dread of the terrible creature, took thought, and answered "Man. In childhood he creeps on hands and knees, in manhood he walks erect, but in old age he has need of a staff."

At this reply the Sphinx uttered a cry, sprang headlong from the rock into the valley below, and perished. Oedipus had guessed the answer. When he came to the city and told the Thebans that their torment was gone, they hailed him as a deliverer. Not long after, they married him with great honor to their widowed queen, Jocasta, his own mother. The destiny was fulfilled.

For years Oedipus lived in peace, unwitting; but at length upon that unhappy city there fell a great pestilence and famine. In his distress the king sent to the Oracle at Delphi, to know what he or the Thebans had done, that they should be so sorely punished. Then for the third time the Oracle spoke his own fateful sentence; and he learned all.

Jocasta died, and Oedipus took the doom upon himself, and left Thebes. Blinded by his own hand, he wandered away into the wilderness. Never again did he rule over men; and he had one only comrade, his faithful daughter Antigone. She was the truest happiness in his life of sorrow, and she never left him till he died.

RECOMMENDED RESOURCES

Robert Fagles, *The Three Theban Plays: Antigone; Oedipus the King; Oedipus at Colonus* (Penguin Classics edition). This edition has an excellent introduction to each play, as well as a good poetic translation. (Note: There is another, older Penguin Classics edition, translated by E.F. Watling, which is adequate but not as good.)

Dudley Fitts and Robert Fitzgerald, *The Oedipus Cycle: Oedipus Rex, Oedipus at Colonus, Antigone.* This is a dynamic and engaging translation.

Sir George Young, *The Theban Plays.* The Dover Thrift Edition is an adequate and inexpensive version, but the translation is a bit stilted.

QUESTIONS FOR DISCUSSION

1. How might the story of *Oedipus Rex* have been different if Oedipus had displayed humility instead of pride at certain critical moments?

2. What is the attraction of pride? Why is it difficult to resist?

3. In the play, Oedipus blinds himself when he finally recognizes the full reality of the situation. Does this indicate repentance? Why or why not?

4. The ancient Greek worldview did not have a place for the forgiveness of sins. How does this affect the outcome of the story?

5. Imagine that time travel allowed a Christian to go back to the setting of *Oedipus Rex*. What could he or she say or do that might change the sequence of events? How might Oedipus respond?

USING THE ARTS

1. Have your group do a dramatic reading of key scenes from *Oedipus Rex.* For a more advanced group, have them adapt the dialogue and characters to a modern setting.

2. View and discuss various artistic depictions of Oedipus, both from his encounter with the Sphinx and dealing with the events of *Oedipus Rex.* How does the painter convey Oedipus? Suggested examples include: *Oedipus and the Sphinx* by Jean-Auguste-Dominique Ingres; *Oedipus and the Sphinx* by Francois-Xavier Fabre; *Oedipus and Antigone, or the Plague of Thebes* by Charles Jalabert; *Blind Oedipus Commending His Children to the Gods* by Bénigne Gagneraux.

The *Aeneid*

Virgil's *Aeneid*, written in 19 BC, is an epic poem in Latin about the founding of Rome. Drawing on the epic tradition of Homer's *Iliad* and *Odyssey*, Virgil (whose name is sometimes spelled Vergil) strives to create a national epic for his fellow Romans. Here, we find the eponymous character Aeneas, a Trojan, fleeing his city after its fall to the Greeks and searching for a new home in Italy, where it is foretold that he will establish a people who will rule the known world.

Although this poem is by a pagan poet, many Christian writers over the centuries have found in Virgil's writings strong foreshadowings of the Christian message, and have found the *Aeneid* to be fruitful as an allegory or image of the Christian life. Dante, in his *Divine Comedy*, even made Virgil into a character who guides the narrator through hell and purgatory.

The *Aeneid* has more of an underlying moral purpose than we saw in the *Odyssey*. In Homer's epic, Odysseus is simply trying to get home; we can readily relate to his goal, but it is self-focused. In contrast, Virgil is telling a story in which the hero, Aeneas, is called to put a divine mission ahead of his own personal desires. We also see a difference in the nature of the characters. As we saw in our discussion of the *Odyssey*, we can admire Odysseus's persistence and cleverness, but he is far from an unambiguously heroic figure in light of the Christian revelation. Aeneas, in contrast, has virtues that are recognizably in congruence with Christianity. Consider, for instance, Aeneas carrying his aged father, Anchises, from the burning ruins of Troy; here we have an act of love and filial piety that a Christian can admire.

However, Aeneas is far from morally perfect, as we see in his treatment of Dido, the queen of Carthage. She falls in love with him, and he spends a night with her, allowing her to believe that he will marry her, but then leaves her behind (secretly) as he and his men sail onward to their hoped-for new home. The brokenhearted Dido, on discovering this betrayal, kills herself.

This moral underpinning combined with the epic journey means that the story of the *Aeneid* is particularly ripe for Christian engagement. We can see this, for instance, in the story's appropriation as a narrative framework: for instance, Ronald Knox titled his story of conversion to Catholicism *A Spiritual Aeneid*.

One of the most important things to realize about the *Aeneid* is that Virgil was deliberately writing it in response to Roman history, and specifically what was for him recent history. He made use of Homeric stories and themes, but recast them as a reflection on war, politics, what it means to found a city, and what it means to be a nation. Thus, the poem as it was written is, in some ways, particularly ripe for reappropriation as a meditation on our journey to a better, heavenly city. It is well worth considering what the story of the *Aeneid* offers to Christians – both for good and for bad.

The story of the *Aeneid* also offers us an opportunity to reflect on the significance of narratives in conveying meaning about the faith. Narratives have a beginning, a middle, and an end, a structure that corresponds to the way that we experience and talk about events in our lives, and our lives as a whole. One of the signals of the human *need* for narrative is that we are dissatisfied when we feel that our lives lack purpose or meaning, or when we do not understand where we have come from, or why we are in the situation we are in. By moving through time and taking the reader with them on the journey, stories provide an incarnational experience that invites connections between story and life.

Thus, it's natural for us to respond to narratives that 'incarnate' or embody important cultural events and cultural values. That's what Virgil is doing: embodying and expressing what he sees as the virtues of Roman culture. So, as we consider the *Aeneid*, we can ask: What truths does Virgil want to convey, and how does he do it? How could we, in the modern day, tell stories that have the kind of cultural impact that the *Aeneid* has had?

Perhaps the most famous section of the *Aeneid* is book VI, sometimes referred to as "The Golden Bough," in which Aeneas descends into the underworld. Here, he speaks with the spirit of his father (who died earlier on the voyage), encounters Dido once more, and receives a prophecy of the future of Rome. We encounter the shades of the dead, in their various circumstances, and it is significant to note that Virgil's depiction of the underworld includes both punishments and rewards for the dead, even though there is no personal, supreme God in this worldview (Jupiter is the king of the Olympian gods, but he is not responsible for the fate of shades in the underworld).

It is interesting to consider the three figures specifically named as being punished in the underworld: Ixion, Sisyphus, and Tantalus. Ixion murdered his father-in-law, was pardoned by Zeus, and later attempted to seduce Hera, Zeus's wife. Sisyphus, a trickster figure, in some stories murdered his guests, seduced his niece, and betrayed one of Zeus's secrets; in others, he cheated death on two occasions. Tantalus murdered his own son and served him as a meal to the gods to test their omniscience; in some stories, he violated Olympian hospitality by stealing nectar and ambrosia, the food of the gods, and bringing it back to his people.

This book of the *Aeneid*, then, is a striking depiction of certain basic human intuitions: that the soul is immortal, that there is objective morality, and that our actions during life will have consequences after death.

SELECTION

Aeneas's journey to the underworld

Excerpt from the prose summary of the *Aeneid* in *The Age of Fable* by Thomas Bulfinch

The ships at last reached the shores of Italy, and joyfully did the adventurers leap to land. While his people were employed in making their encampment Aeneas sought the abode of the Sibyl. It was a cave connected with a temple and grove, sacred to Apollo and Diana. While Aeneas contemplated the scene, the Sibyl accosted him. She seemed to know his errand, and under the influence of the deity of the place, burst forth in a prophetic strain, giving dark intimations of labors and perils through which he was destined to make his way to final success. She closed with the encouraging words which have become proverbial: "Yield not to disasters, but press onward the more bravely." Aeneas replied that he had prepared himself for whatever might await him. He had but one request to make. Having been directed in a dream to seek the abode of the dead in order to confer with his father, Anchises, to receive from him a revelation of his future fortunes and those of his race, he asked her assistance to enable him to accomplish the task. The Sibyl replied, "The descent to Avernus is easy: the gate of Pluto stands open night and day; but to retrace one's steps and return to the upper air, that is the toil, that the difficulty." She instructed him to seek in the forest a tree on which grew a golden branch. This branch was to be plucked off and borne as a gift to Proserpine, and if fate was propitious it would yield to the hand and quit its parent trunk, but otherwise no force could rend it away. If torn away, another would succeed.

Aeneas followed the directions of the Sibyl. His mother, Venus, sent two of her doves to fly before him and show him the way, and by their assistance he found the tree, plucked the branch, and hastened back with it to the Sibyl.

"Now," said the Sibyl, "summon up your courage, for you will need it." She descended into the cave [of Avernus], and Aeneas followed.... They then came to the black river Cocytus, where they found the ferryman, Charon, old and squalid, but strong and vigorous, who was receiving passengers of all kinds into his boat.... They stood pressing for a passage and longing to touch the opposite shore. But the stern ferryman took in only such as he chose, driving the rest back. Aeneas, wondering at the sight, asked the Sibyl, "Why this discrimination?" She answered, "Those who are taken on board the bark are the souls of those who have received due burial rites; the host of others who have remained unburied are not permitted to pass the flood, but wander a hundred years, and flit to and fro about the shore, till at last they are taken over." . . .

Charon, fixing his eyes sternly upon the advancing warrior, demanded by what right he, living and armed, approached that shore. To which the Sibyl replied that they would commit no violence, that Aeneas's only object was to see his father, and finally exhibited the golden branch, at sight of which Charon's wrath relaxed, and he made haste to turn his bark to the shore, and receive them on board. The boat, adapted only to the light freight of bodiless spirits, groaned under the weight of the hero. They were soon conveyed to the opposite shore. . . . The first sound that struck their ears was the wailing of young children, who had died on the threshold of life, and near to these were they who had perished under false charges. Minos presides over them as judge, and examines the deeds of each. The next class was of those who had died by their own hand, hating life and seeking refuge in death. O how willingly would they now endure poverty, labor, and any other infliction, if they might but return to life! Next were situated the regions of sadness, divided off into retired paths, leading through groves of myrtle. Here roamed those who had fallen victims to unrequited love, not freed from pain even by death itself. Among these, Aeneas thought he descried the form of Dido, with a wound still recent. In the dim light he was for a moment uncertain, but approaching, perceived it was indeed herself. Tears fell from his eyes, and he addressed her in the accents of love. "Unhappy Dido! was then the rumor true that you had perished? and was I, alas! the cause? I call the gods to witness that my departure from you was reluctant, and in obedience to the commands of Jove; nor could I believe that my absence would cost you so dear. Stop, I beseech you, and refuse me not a last farewell." She stood for a moment with averted countenance, and eyes fixed on the ground, and then silently passed on, as insensible to his pleadings as a rock. Aeneas followed for some distance; then, with a heavy heart, rejoined his companion and resumed his route.

They next entered the fields where roam the heroes who have fallen in battle. Here they saw many shades of Grecian and Trojan warriors. The Trojans thronged around him, and could not be satisfied with the sight. They asked the cause of his coming, and plied him with innumerable questions. . . .

Aeneas would have lingered long with his Trojan friends, but the Sibyl hurried him away. They next came to a place where the road divided, the one leading to Elysium, the other to the regions of the condemned. Aeneas beheld on one side the walls of a mighty city, around which Phlegethon rolled its fiery waters. Before him was the gate of adamant that neither gods nor men can break through. An iron tower stood by the gate, on which Tisiphone, the avenging Fury, kept guard. From the city were heard groans, and the sound of the scourge, the creaking of iron, and the clanking of chains. Aeneas, horror-struck, inquired of his guide what crimes were those whose punishments produced the sounds he heard? The Sibyl answered, "Here is the judgment hall of Rhadamanthus, who brings to light crimes done in life, which the perpetrator vainly thought impenetrably hid. Tisiphone applies her whip of scorpions, and delivers the offender over to her sister Furies." . . .

Aeneas saw groups seated at tables loaded with dainties, while near by stood a Fury who snatched away the viands from their lips as fast as they prepared to taste them. Others beheld suspended over their heads huge rocks, threatening to fall, keeping them in a state of constant alarm. These were they who had hated their brothers, or struck their parents, or defrauded the friends who trusted them, or who, having grown rich, kept their money to themselves, and gave no share to others; the last being the most numerous class. Here also were those who had violated the marriage vow, or fought in a bad cause, or failed in fidelity to their employers. Here was one who had sold his country for gold, another who perverted the laws, making them say one thing to-day and another to-morrow.

Ixion was there, fastened to the circumference of a wheel ceaselessly revolving; and Sisyphus, whose task was to roll a huge stone up to a hill-top, but when the steep was well-nigh gained, the rock, repulsed by some sudden force, rushed again headlong down to the plain. Again he toiled at it, while the sweat bathed all his weary limbs, but all to no effect. There was Tantalus, who stood in a pool, his chin level with the water, yet he was parched with thirst, and found nothing to assuage it; for when he bowed his hoary head, eager to quaff, the water fled away, leaving the ground at his feet all dry. Tall trees laden with fruit stooped their heads to him, pears, pomegranates, apples, and luscious figs; but when with a sudden grasp he tried to seize them winds whirled them high above his reach.

The Sibyl now warned Aeneas that it was time to turn from these melancholy regions and seek the city of the blessed. They passed through a middle tract of darkness, and came upon the Elysian fields, the groves where the happy reside. They breathed a freer air, and saw all objects clothed in a purple light. The region has a sun and stars of its own. The inhabitants were enjoying themselves in various ways, some in sports on the grassy turf, in games of strength or skill, others dancing or singing. Orpheus struck the chords of his lyre, and called forth ravishing sounds. Here Aeneas saw the founders of the Trojan state, magnanimous heroes who lived in happier times. He gazed with admiration on the war chariots and glittering arms now reposing in disuse. Spears stood fixed in the ground, and the horses, unharnessed, roamed over the plain. The same pride in splendid armor and generous steeds which the old heroes felt in life, accompanied them here. He saw another group feasting and listening to the strains of music. They were in a laurel grove, whence the great river Po has its origin, and flows out among men. Here dwelt those who fell by wounds received in their country's cause, holy priests also, and poets who have uttered thoughts worthy of Apollo, and others who have contributed to cheer and adorn life by their discoveries in the useful arts, and have made their memory blessed by rendering service to mankind. They wore snow-white fillets about their brows. The Sibyl addressed a group of these, and inquired where Anchises was to be found. They were directed where to seek him, and soon found him in a verdant valley, where he was contemplating the ranks of his posterity, their destinies and worthy deeds to be achieved in coming times. When he recognized Aeneas approaching, he stretched out both hands to him, while tears flowed freely. "Have you come at last," said he, "long expected, and do I behold you after such perils past? O my son, how have I trembled for you as I have watched your career!" To which Aeneas replied, "O father! your image was always before me to guide and guard me." Then he endeavored to enfold his father in his embrace, but his arms enclosed only an unsubstantial image.

Aeneas perceived before him a spacious valley, with trees gently waving to the wind, a tranquil landscape, through which the river Lethe flowed. Along the banks of the stream wandered a countless multitude, numerous as insects in the summer air. Aeneas, with surprise, inquired who were these. Anchises answered, "They are souls to which bodies are to be given in due time. Meanwhile they dwell on Lethe's bank, and drink oblivion of their former lives." . . .

Anchises, having explained so much, proceeded to point out to Aeneas individuals of his race, who were hereafter to be born, and to relate to him the exploits they should perform in the world. After this he reverted to the present, and told his son of the events that remained to him to be accomplished before the complete establishment of himself and his followers in Italy. Wars were to be waged, battles fought, a bride to be won, and in the result a Trojan state founded, from which should rise the Roman power, to be in time the sovereign of the world.

Aeneas and the Sibyl then took leave of Anchises, and returned by some short cut, which the poet does not explain, to the upper world.

RECOMMENDED RESOURCES

Robert Fagles, *The Aeneid* (Penguin Classics). Fagles's translation is excellent, and the Penguin Classics and Penguin Classics Deluxe editions have useful introductions as well.

Sarah Ruden, *The Aeneid.* Her translation is poetically strong and readable, and the revised and expanded edition from Yale University Press has a helpful introduction and glossary.

C.S. Lewis, *C.S. Lewis's Lost Aeneid: Arms and the Exile*, ed. A.T. Reyes. This is an edition of Lewis's partial translation of the *Aeneid.*

Ronald Knox, *A Spiritual Aeneid: Being an Account of a Journey to the Catholic Faith.*

C.S. Lewis, *A Preface to Paradise Lost.* The entire discussion of epic poetry is helpful, and in chapters VI and VII, Lewis specifically discusses Virgil and the "secondary epic."

C.S. Lewis, *The Abolition of Man*, and Michael Ward, *After Humanity: A Guide to C.S. Lewis's The Abolition of Man.* Lewis's book offers a profound defense of the reality of objective value: that there is such a thing as right and wrong, which all human beings can know, whether or not they are Christians or even theists. Ward's book provides a clear and helpful explanation of this important but difficult and complex text.

QUESTIONS FOR DISCUSSION

1. Compare Aeneas to Odysseus. What are his heroic qualities? What are his weaknesses?

2. Compare Dido to Penelope, Odysseus's wife who fends off her suitors while waiting many years for her husband to return. Is Dido morally stronger or weaker than Penelope?

3. In what way does the *Aeneid* depict the theological virtue of hope? In what way might this be limited by its pre-Christian context?

4. Reflecting on your own spiritual journey, would you describe it more as a "Spiritual Odyssey" or as a "Spiritual Aeneid"? Why?

5. Consider the punishments meted out to Ixion, Sisyphus, and Tantalus in the underworld. Are these punishments just? Why or why not?

6. How is Virgil's underworld similar to the Christian understanding of hell and heaven? How is it different?

7. A 'national epic' or 'national mythology' can have a profound effect in forming identity and culture. When the narrative is a healthy one and is assimilated properly, this can provide a positive sense of shared values. However, if the narrative is built on principles that are not consistent with the Gospel, or if it is made an end in itself, it can become dangerous and even idolatrous. How can Christians ensure that our cultural narratives operate in a Christ-centered way?

8. What is the place of objective morality (what C.S. Lewis called the *Tao*) in Virgil's *Aeneid*? How is the pagan worldview of Virgil different from a 'post-Christian' paganism in the modern day?

9. Aeneas leaves Dido behind in obedience to Jupiter, who reminds him of his mission to establish a city in Italy; this can be interpreted in Christian terms, as placing obedience to God's call above human relationships, and therefore seems to place Aeneas in a positive light. However, the situation in the *Aeneid* is more complicated than this reading might suggest. Did Aeneas treat Dido with justice and charity? Could he have acted differently and still followed his mission? Did he use his mission as an excuse to avoid dealing with the consequences of his entanglement with Dido? Consider these questions and apply them to questions of Christian vocation and relationships.

USING THE ARTS

1. The tale of Dido and Aeneas is one of the most famous tragic love stories in literature. Have students create a script and act out key scenes from their story, such as their meeting, Dido's death, and their encounter in the underworld. For more advanced groups, consider having them write an alternate ending to the story of Dido and Aeneas.

2. Have participants each draw a map to represent their own spiritual journey. Where have they been, where are they, where are they headed?

3. Have participants set up a mock podcast/video where a host interviews various characters from the *Aeneid*, played by different people in the group. Note: This activity is great for getting young people to engage fully with each character in a fun way, but it can turn into parody or silliness if not properly guided. I recommend that you allow for it to be gently tongue-in-cheek in performance, as this allows students to let their guard down a bit, but make sure to return to discussing serious themes and insights from the activity afterward.

Chapter Four

MEDIEVAL LITERATURE

Backgrounds and Context: Allegory

As we move from the ancient into the medieval world, our literary atmosphere changes. All our selections in the Ancient section were written by pagan authors, before the birth of Christ. The selections in the rest of this book are all written by Christians (and indeed, by Catholics, as before the Protestant Reformation, to be a Christian in the West was to be a Catholic). We now have a shared faith with the authors of our selections, but we should be prepared for a different kind of strangeness: that of familiar things seen from a very different angle.

One notable literary difference is the prevalence of allegory in medieval literature. We will encounter it in several of our selections. It is a form that has fallen so far out of use in the modern day that most readers have a great deal of difficulty recognizing it and appreciating it. However, it is a rewarding form when it's properly understood, so we'll take some time here to consider it and be well prepared for our journey through medieval literature.

In the literary form of allegory, the text is intended to operate on two levels, the literal and the allegorical (the allegorical level can be further subdivided, but this need not concern us here). First, we have the *literal* level, in which the story works on its own with its plot, characters, setting, and so on. Second, we have the *allegorical* level, in which the characters, places, and events of the literal level serve to present and illuminate another idea. The two levels can be summed up as 'what the story is about' and 'what ideas the author is presenting in the story.' It is important to note that literary allegories are intentionally created by their author to have these two levels (they are not accidental), and the interpretation of the allegory's significance is intended by the author to be objective and discoverable by the reader (not a subjective meaning invented or imposed by the reader).

An allegory can address a religious, philosophical, political, or social topic – indeed, it can be about anything at all. One of the most famous allegories in literature is the seventeenth-century *Pilgrim's Progress* by John Bunyan, in which the character, Christian, represents (as his name suggests) an ordinary Christian; his journey and adventures stand for the challenges faced by Christians in their lives. The names of the places en route, such as the Slough of Despond and Vanity Fair, clearly signal the allegorical connections; the story is an engaging adventure that is also, and primarily, about resisting the temptations of the world and getting to heaven.

Another significant allegory is the fourteenth-century epic the *Divine Comedy*, by Dante Alighieri. Dante himself explained, in a letter to his patron, that the subject of the poem as a whole "taken merely in the literal sense is 'the state of the soul after death straightforwardly affirmed,' for the development of the whole work hinges on and about that. But if, indeed, the work is taken allegorically, its subject is: 'Man, as by good or ill deserts, in the exercise of his free choice, he becomes liable to rewarding or punishing Justice.'"[1]

A modern example is George Orwell's novel *Animal Farm*, which is a political allegory about totalitarianism. On one level, *Animal Farm* is a beast-fable: it's the story of farmyard animals who revolt against their human master and set up their own rule, which then goes badly. It's possible to read the book and only notice the literal level, with the characters of horses and pigs and so on in their struggles. But what *Animal Farm* is really about is totalitarianism: its false promises and dangerous results.

In order to be an allegory, the connection between the two levels (story and meaning) must operate through the entire work, not just parts of it. Keeping this in mind will help us avoid forcing allegorical meanings on works that aren't, in fact, intended as allegories and thereby misunderstanding or distorting the work.

For instance, C.S. Lewis's *The Lion, the Witch and the Wardrobe* is *not* an allegory. Rather, it is an exploration of who Christ is, worked out via the imaginative 'what if' or 'supposal' of "What if Christ were incarnate in another world?" Certain elements, such as the death and resurrection of Aslan, correspond closely to the scriptural accounts, but there is no one-to-one correspondence with the life of Christ, or the Gospels, in the tale overall. The Christian themes and ideas are profoundly present – indeed, Lewis said that the Narnia Chronicles were "about Christ" – but the literary mode in which these ideas are present is not allegory. (In contrast, Lewis did write an allegorical novel, *The Pilgrim's Regress*.) Similarly,

---

1. Dante Alighieri, *Letter to Can Grande*, quoted in Dorothy Sayers, introduction to *The Divine Comedy Part 1: Hell*, by Dante Alighieri (New York: Penguin, 1950), 14–15.

J.R.R. Tolkien's *The Lord of the Rings* is not an allegory, though it certainly has what Tolkien himself called "applicability."

Recognizing and following allegory is harder for us modern readers than it would have been for readers in the medieval through early modern period. Allegory was once a popular and easily understood literary form, recognized by readers in the same way that we can easily see the difference between a historical novel and a historical nonfiction book. But since it has fallen out of favor, and become unfamiliar to most readers, it takes a certain amount of work to get into the allegorical mindset.

In order to appreciate an allegory, we need to be aware of both levels of the story at (more or less) the same time, allowing each level to enhance our appreciation of the other. Indeed, the whole point of an allegory is the interaction between the two levels. In the best allegories, the two levels are never entirely separable; the images chosen by the poet are more than simple markers for ideas.

Allegory is significant for our engagement with medieval literature in general because it points to the medieval Christian way of viewing the world as an integrated whole, in which *everything* has meaning. Many aspects of reality that we moderns tend to put into separate, and often opposing, categories (such as imagination and reason, the spiritual world and the material world, scientific facts and moral values) were held together in the medieval mind. To the credit side of the modern day, we have gained much scientific and practical knowledge over the last few centuries, and the Church has continued to unfold the meaning of the deposit of faith, giving us a fuller understanding of doctrine. But we have also lost some of the wisdom that our medieval brothers and sisters had; their faith was, at its best, more fully integrated into their lives, and more fully incarnational in its practice, than our own tends to be in the twenty-first century. There is much that we can learn from them.

“The Dream of the Rood”

We begin our journey into medieval literature with the “Dream of the Rood” – one of the best poems that you’ve probably never heard of. This Old English poem tells the story of the Crucifixion from the point of view of the cross; the word ‘rood’ means ‘cross.’ This poem, by an unnamed poet, was written sometime between the eighth century and its recording in the tenth-century Vercelli Book manuscript. Whatever its exact date, it is one of the oldest and most significant poems in Old English literature; there may even be a quote from it inscribed on the eighth-century Ruthwell Cross.

The poet uses a distinctive literary device, setting up the poem as a dream vision. By using this framing device, the poet is making it clear that this is an imaginative interpretation of the Crucifixion, not a straight telling of it; it gives him freedom to convey the meaning in fresh ways.

The account we find here matches the Apostles’ Creed and the Nicene Creed: in the poem, Jesus is fully God and fully man; he is crucified, dies, is buried, rises, ascends, and will come again in judgment. But this structurally sophisticated poem is more than a poetic recitation of doctrine. The poem has three parts. First, the poet tells of his dream, describes the cross, and reflects on his response to the sight of the cross. Second, the cross itself speaks, recounts the events of the Crucifixion, Resurrection, and Ascension of Christ, and describes Christ’s future coming in judgment. Finally, the poet reflects on his dream and on his current situation, resolves to seek the salvation of the cross (that is, of Christ crucified), and concludes in hope and praise.

The structure of the poem thus moves the reader naturally from reflection on the life, death, and Resurrection of Christ to prayer and a personal resolution to strive for holiness.

The poem tells the story of the Crucifixion as if Christ were a young warrior climbing onto the cross, presenting the Gospel account in a way that would resonate with the pagan heroic culture. Christ does indeed do battle with death and sin! It is also an excellent way, in our modern culture, of challenging faulty ideas about our Lord that are so deep-seated as to be invisible at first. In my teaching of this poem, I’ve found that my Christian students often recognize here for the first time that their image of Jesus on the cross is as a passive victim, not an active Savior; that their grasp of the redemption won for us on the cross is a purely abstract concept, disconnected from a sense of the flesh-and-blood reality of Jesus. "The Dream of the Rood" shakes that up and helps them to see the Passion narrative with fresh eyes.

"The Dream of the Rood" also provides a natural opening to discuss prayer to the saints. In the poem, not only is the cross personified and given a speaking part, but the narrator *prays* to it. For Protestant readers, this can seem like an endorsement of idolatry – which is what they fear that Catholics commit when we pray to Mary and the saints. Even for Catholics, there can be a lot of confusion (and even, at times, some superstition) related to the intercession of the saints, so the situation presented in this poem allows for a thoughtful discussion of intercessory prayer.

Today, we usually make a sharp distinction between praying *for* someone (praying to God on their behalf) and praying *to* someone – the latter being rightly directed to God alone. But the older usage of "to pray" meant simply to make an earnest request of someone: to pray God for mercy, to pray the king for help, to pray one's friend to lend a hand, and so on. This usage has been almost entirely lost today, though we can see it in archaic forms that still appear in the occasional historical novel: "Prithee come to mine house for a meal, friend!" (Prithee = 'I pray thee' = 'I ask you'). When Catholics offer prayer *to* Mary and the saints, we are asking for their intercession and help in exactly the same way, and for the same reason, that we ask fellow living Christians for prayer and assistance: because God created us to be in community and to support each other. In his wisdom, and in a mysterious way, God acts both directly and through the intercession of his saints.

But, we might object, this distinction doesn't apply here, because the cross isn't a person. On the literary level, we can address this by noting that the rood has been *personified* as a living being capable of intercession. In waking, nonpoetic life, the poet would pray to Christ on the cross, or perhaps ask the Blessed Mother or St. John, who were present at the Crucifixion, to intercede for him. Thus, the poet is not depicting or endorsing idolatry. His use of the dream framework underscores that he *intends* us to interpret these events figuratively and imaginatively.

The poet's prayer to the personified-rood-as-saint also reminds us of the way that the ordinary cross or crucifix in their local church or home points toward Christ crucified and reminds us of what our Lord did for us to save us from our sin. In this way, "The Dream of the Rood" provides a valuable opportunity to talk about the veneration of icons and relics.

The Catholic custom of the Adoration (or Veneration) of the Cross on Good Friday is ancient; it began with St. Helena's discovery of the relic of the true cross in Jerusalem in the fourth century and became a widespread practice in other churches in the seventh century. Thus, the Rood-poet would almost certainly have participated in the Adoration of the Cross during the Good Friday liturgy – the same devotional practice that we have today, though more than a thousand years separate his day from ours.

In the Adoration of the Cross, we bow or genuflect to a crucifix that is held up before us and we also kiss or reverently touch it. It can feel awkward; we may be uneasy about touching with our lips or hand something that other lips have touched (even though we have already touched door handles, pews, hymnals, and so on). For many Catholics, it may seem slightly pointless or even vulgar. But, in fact, it is a deeply meaningful action – if we understand it rightly.

This act of veneration is a tangible way of expressing our gratitude and love for our Lord's death for us. It is an embodiment of the literary device of *synecdoche*: using the part to stand for the whole. A crucifix is a visual image of our Lord's death upon the cross, which in turn stands for our entire salvation, won for us by his death. The significance of the cross is pointed out explicitly in the Good Friday liturgy. At the beginning of the Adoration of the Cross, the priest announces, "Behold the wood of the Cross, on which hung the salvation of the world." A later antiphon for the Adoration runs, "We adore your Cross, O Lord, we praise and glorify your holy Resurrection, for behold, because of the wood of a tree joy has come to the whole world." Venerating the cross thus allows us imaginatively to deepen our understanding of, and gratitude for, our salvation.

Thus far we have only considered the basic premise of the poem: the centrality of the cross, and its role as a narrator in the poem. We should now consider how the poet has imaginatively adapted the story of the Crucifixion to his contemporary setting.

Christ's burial, in the poem, comes across as more dignified and formal than it was in actual history, but this modification is within the range of acceptable imaginative depictions of the historical event; we should keep in mind that the poem is explicitly presented as a dream-vision. The poem describes a burial and dirge along the lines of a Viking burial of a fallen hero; by presenting Our Lord as a warrior, the poet strengthens the effect of the Crucifixion for his audience. For a pagan, the idea of a king or mighty warrior going willingly to suffer humiliating torture and death would be shocking and repellent; it underscores the message of the Gospel, that the values of this world have been turned upside down. Humility, not worldly honor, is the characteristic of life in this kingdom.

Oddly enough, in the modern day, we have in some ways reverted to this pagan perspective. Modern people in the West tend to avoid even thinking about death, disability, and illness. Indeed, the disturbing rise of so-called assisted suicide and euthanasia suggests that many people fear disability, weakness, dependency, and pain far more than death.

"The Dream of the Rood" works to reorient the reader's values: here we see heroism and glory, but it is a new kind of heroism, a new kind of glory. On the surface, without considering its significance, Christ's death is unheroic and repellent; we modern Christians tend to forget just how degrading a crucifixion was, and how much it undermines conventional ideas of strength and leadership. Our Lord's body had to be cleaned and anointed when it was taken down from the cross; there was blood and fluid from the wounds in his hands and side, as well as sweat, blood, dirt, and bruises from his scourging, the carrying of the cross, and his falls along the way. This is a significant part of the 'offensiveness' of the Gospel: not just the recognition of one's own sin but the awareness of the particular means by which our sin is forgiven.

How do we grasp that this humiliating death was actually a cosmic victory and that the naked man nailed to a tree is the Lord of lords and King of kings? The Rood-poet gives it a try, not just in the picture of Christ as the young warrior, but in the surreal dream-vision imagery of the cross itself at the start of the poem. It is richly decorated, with five gems on the crossbeam and others scattered at its foot. What we are seeing is a representation of Christ's blood, staining the cross itself from his five wounds and dropped onto the ground when his side was pierced by the centurion's spear. It is the blood of God Incarnate, the blood by which we are saved – a single drop is infinitely more precious than anything on earth. When we receive this very same blood in the sacrament of the Eucharist, it is hidden from our senses by the veil of the consecrated bread and wine. It is the poet's gift to us to show us, in this imagery, something of the reality we cannot yet see with our eyes.

SELECTION

"The Dream of the Rood"

The full poem, from *Old English Poems Translated into the Original Meter*, edited by Cosette Faust and Stith Thompson

Lo, I shall tell you the truest of visions,
A dream that I dreamt in the dead of night
While people reposed in peaceful sleep.
I seemed to see the sacred tree
Lifted on high in a halo of light,
The brightest of beams; that beacon was wholly
Gorgeous with gold; glorious gems stood
Fair at the foot; and five were assembled,
At the crossing of the arms. The angels of God looked on,
Fair through the firmament. It was truly no foul sinner's cross,
For beholding his sufferings were the holy spirits,
The men of the earth and all of creation.
Wondrous was that victory-wood, and I wounded and stained
With sorrows and sins. I saw the tree of glory
Blessed and bright in brilliant adornments,
Made joyous with jewels. Gems on all sides
Full rarely enriched the rood of the Savior.
Through the sight of that cross I came to perceive
Its stiff struggle of old, when it started first
To bleed on the right side. I was broken and cast down with sorrow;
The fair sight inspired me with fear. Before me the moving beacon
Changed its clothing and color. At times it was covered with blood
Fearful and grimy with gore. At times with gold 'twas adorned.
Then I lay and looked for a long time
And saw the Savior's sorrowful tree
Until I heard it lift high its voice.

The worthiest of the wood-race formed words and spoke:
"It was ages ago – I shall always remember –

When first I was felled at the forest's edge,
My strong trunk stricken. Then strange enemies took me
And fashioned my frame to a cross; and their felons I raised on high.
On their backs and shoulders they bore me to the brow of the lofty hill.
There the hated ones solidly set me. I saw there the Lord of Mankind
Struggling forward with courage to climb my sturdy trunk.
I dared not then oppose the purpose of the Lord,
So I bent not nor broke when there burst forth a trembling
From the ends of the earth. Easily might I
Destroy the murderers, but I stood unmoved.
"The Young Hero unclothed him – it was the holy God –
Strong and steadfast; he stepped to the high gallows,
Not fearing the look of the fiends, and there he freed mankind.
At his blessed embrace I trembled, but bow to the earth I dared not,
Or forward to fall to the ground, but fast and true I endured.
As a rood I was raised up; a royal King I bore,
The Lord of heavenly legions. I allowed myself never to bend.
Dark nails through me they drove; so that dastardly scars are upon me,
Wounds wide open; but not one of them dared I to harm.
They cursed and reviled us together. I was covered all over with blood,
That flowed from the Savior's side when his soul had left the flesh.
Sorrowful the sights I have seen on that hill,
Grim-visaged grief: the God of mankind I saw
And his frightful death. The forces of darkness
Covered with clouds the corpse of the Lord,
The shining radiance; the shadows darkened
Under the cover of clouds. Creation all wept,
The king's fall bewailed. Christ was on the rood.
Finally from afar came faithful comrades
To the Savior's side, and I saw it all.
Bitter the grief that I bore, but I bowed me low to their hands;
My travail was grievous and sore. They took then God Almighty,
From loathsome torment they lifted him. The warriors left me deserted,
To stand stained with blood. I was stricken and wounded with nails.
Limb-weary they laid him there, and at their Lord's head they stood.
They beheld there the Ruler of heaven; and they halted a while to rest,
Tired after the terrible struggle. A tomb then they began to make,

His friends in sight of his foes. Of the fairest of stone they built it,
And set their Savior upon it. A sorrowful dirge they chanted,
Lamented their Master at evening, when they made their journey home,
Tired from their loved Lord's side. And they left him with the guard.
We crosses stood there streaming with blood,
And waited long after the wailing ceased
Of thc brave company. The body grew cold,
The most precious of corpses. Then they pulled us down,
All to the earth – an awful fate!
They buried us low in a pit. But the loved disciples of Christ,
His faithful friends made search and found me and brought me to light,
And gorgeously decked me with gold and with silver.

"Now mayst thou learn, my beloved friend,
That the work of the wicked I have worthily borne,
The most trying of torments. The time is now come
When through the wide world I am worshipped and honored,
That all manner of men, and the mighty creation,
Hold sacred this sign. On me the Son of God
Death-pangs endured. Hence, dauntless in glory,
I rise high under heaven, and hold out salvation
To each and to all who have awe in my presence.

"Long ago I was the greatest and most grievous of torments,
Most painful of punishments, till I pointed aright
The road of life for the race of men.

"Lo, a glory was given by the God of Creation
To the worthless wood – by the Warden of heaven –
Just as Mary, his mother, the maiden blessed,
Received grace and glory from God Almighty,
And homage and worship over other women.

"And now I bid thee, my best of comrades,
That thou reveal this vision to men.
Tell them I am truly the tree of glory,
That the Savior sorrowed and suffered upon me
For the race of men and its many sins,
And the ancient evil that Adam wrought.

"He there tasted of death; but in triumph he rose,
The Lord in his might and gave life unto men.
Then he ascended to heaven, and hither again
Shall the Savior descend to seek mankind

On the day of doom, the dreaded Ruler
Of highest heaven, with his host of angels.
Then will he adjudge with justice and firmness
Rewards to the worthy whose works have deserved them,
Who loyally lived their lives on the earth.
Then a feeling of fear shall fill every heart
For the warning they had in the words of their Master:
He shall demand of many where the man may be found
To consent for the sake of his Savior to taste
The bitter death as He did on the cross.
They are filled with fear and few of them think
What words they shall speak in response to Christ.
Then no feeling of fright or fear need he have
Who bears on his heart the brightest of tokens,
But there shall come to the kingdom through the cross and its power
All the souls of the saved from the sorrows of earth,
Of the holy who hope for a home with their Lord."

Then I adored the cross with undaunted courage,
With the warmest zeal, while I watched alone
And saw it in secret. My soul was eager
To depart on its path, but I have passed through many
An hour of longing. Through all my life
I shall seek the sight of that sacred tree
Alone more often than all other men
And worthily worship it. My will for this service
Is steadfast and sturdy, and my strength is ever
In the cross of Christ. My comrades of old,
The friends of fortune, all far from the earth
Have departed from the world and its pleasures
        and have passed to the King of Glory,
And high in the heavens with the holy God
Are living eternally. And I long for the time
To arrive at last when the rood of the Lord,
Which once so plainly appeared to my sight,
Shall summon my soul from this sorrowful life,
And bring me to that bourne where bliss is unending
And happiness of heaven, where the holy saints
All join in a banquet, where joy is eternal.

May He set me where always in after time
I shall dwell in glory with God's chosen ones
In delights everlasting. May the Lord be my friend,
Who came to earth and of old on the cross
Suffered and sorrowed for the sins of men.
He broke there our bonds and bought for us life
And a heavenly home. The hearts were now filled
With blessings and bliss, which once burned with remorse.
To the Son was his journey successful and joyful
And crowned with triumph, when he came with his troops,
With his gladsome guests into God's kingdom,
The Almighty Judge's, and brought joy to the angels,
And the host of the holy who in heaven before
Dwelt in glory when their God arrived,
The Lord Most High, at his home at last.

RECOMMENDED RESOURCES

Though it is in English, "The Dream of the Rood" is in *Old* English, which is so different from modern English that it must be read in translation. Some translations render it into prose; my strong preference is for a poetic translation. Since the poem is too short to be published by itself, print versions will be found in anthologies.

Kevin Crossley-Holland, translator and editor, *The Anglo-Saxon World: An Anthology* (Oxford World's Classics). This volume is my go-to choice for Old English literature. It includes "The Dream of the Rood" in a good poetic translation, and the other texts are also handed well (with the exception of *Beowulf*: the translation of it here is plodding). The introductions to the various texts are short, clear, and helpful.

Richard Hamer, editor, *A Choice of Anglo-Saxon Verse*, revised and expanded edition (Faber). This volume provides an excellent translation with the original Old English reproduced on facing pages. The introduction is brief, however.

Michael Alexander, editor, *The First Poems in English* (Penguin Classics). This edition gives a prose translation, so I don't suggest it as your main source. However, the ample supporting explanatory material by Alexander is very good. It can also be useful to have a prose version to use comparatively for understanding the poem.

Malcolm Guite, "Seeing Through Dreams: Image and Truth in *The Dream of the Rood*," in *Faith, Hope and Poetry: Theology and the Poetic Imagination.*

QUESTIONS FOR DISCUSSION

1. Gems and gold were greatly valued by early medieval English culture; a good ruler was called a "gold-giver" or "ring-giver." What does the image of the jeweled cross tell us about Jesus?

2. Jesus is fully human and fully divine, and therefore he is the *perfect* man in every respect. How does Christianity challenge a "macho" view of masculinity?

3. What is your usual mental image of Christ? Does "The Dream of the Rood" change that image? If so, how?

4. What is the effect of having the cross narrate the story of the Crucifixion? What insights do we gain from seeing this familiar story from such a surprising point of view?

5. How is the symbolism of the jewels different from the synecdoche of the cross itself? Why is the Eucharist *not* merely a symbol?

6. What is the meaning conveyed by a crucifix as opposed to a bare cross? How would you respond to the objection that a crucifix is too focused on the death of Christ and not on the Resurrection?

USING THE ARTS

1. Find artwork that displays the cross in dream-vision style; this may include crucifixes that show the risen Christ and altar crosses that are made with gold and jewels. Then find images of very realistic crucifixes. Compare and discuss. What does each style tell us about the reality of the Crucifixion? What is the complete picture that these different images are contributing to?

2. Assign the participants in your group to research the imagery and symbolism of various items and actions used in worship, such as the vessels for consecration being made of precious metal, the use of candles, the priest kissing the altar and the Gospel book, the monstrance used for Adoration of the Blessed Sacrament, and so on. Then, in a later session, discuss how each of these helps us to understand more of the meaning of our faith. (Note: It's best not to assume that anyone knows what the symbolism means ahead of time. If you can't assign independent research, I recommend preparing a handout with some examples – preferably ones that can be seen in your own church – to support the discussion.)

3. Draw a picture of the cross, the empty tomb, or the instruments of crucifixion (hammer, nails, spear) in a dream-vision manner that shows them in the light of their spiritual significance.

Beowulf

Our next venture into the medieval world is the marvelous adventure of *Beowulf.* This poem offers the reader monsters, dragons, and exciting battles, as well as powerful insights into human nature, sin, and virtue.

Here we find the monster Grendel, sick with envy and hate as he lurks outside Heorot Hall and hears the warriors celebrating within. Night after night, he attacks the hall and murders the warriors, until the mighty Beowulf arrives, volunteering to help. He defeats Grendel in single combat, and then tracks the dying monster back to his underwater lair in the wilderness. There, he also defeats Grendel's rage-filled mother, ending the monsters' reign of terror. Then, years later, we find that Beowulf is now the honored leader of his people – and they are now threatened by a dragon, which is wreaking vengeance on the countryside after a single cup was stolen from its hoard. The aging Beowulf brings a picked band of men to fight the dragon, but at the last minute declares that he will fight alone. His sword breaks and he is mortally wounded, but the warrior Wiglaf comes to his aid and kills the dragon.

"Old" stories aren't boring stories!

It's easy to assume that a poem with so much heroic monster-fighting would present a one-dimensional picture of masculinity, but this is, interestingly, not the case. Beowulf is challenged by the snarky and resentful Unferth – but rather than escalating the conflict into a brawl, Beowulf handles the situation with calm confidence, and eventually we see Unferth won over to supporting Beowulf. Offering a balance to Beowulf's brash strength is Hrothgar, the ruler of Heorot, who is respected even though he's unable himself to defeat Grendel. Hrothgar dishes out a lot of salutary advice to Beowulf about *not* becoming overconfident or prideful after his victory. Beowulf himself displays true humility in his fight with Grendel. He doesn't pretend that he isn't any stronger or better as a warrior than the other men; that would be *false* humility, because he really does have exceptional strength. His humility rests in recognizing that it is not through his own merits, but as a gift from God, that he is strong.

Interestingly, the poet rounds out the picture of the heroic-and-humble Beowulf as a young man with Beowulf as a mature leader. Although he is honored as a great leader, we see that Beowulf isn't quite as resistant to the sin of pride as he was in his youth. His decision to take on the dragon singlehandedly looks a lot like an attempt to recapture his youthful glory days. As is usually the case, this fails. Teamwork, not egotistical posing, saves the day.

We see, then, that Beowulf is a three-dimensional character of his own, with his own virtues and faults. He is also a Christ-figure. His descent into the dark water of the mere to fight Grendel's mother is an image of Christ's death and also of baptism. The danger and fearfulness of it in the poem helps us to see afresh what baptism means.

One of the most fruitful ways of exploring this great poem is by considering the *applicability* of the characters and events to our understanding of sin and virtue. The poem is not an allegory, but there are many thematic connections to Christian themes in the characters, situations, and imagery.

Grendel, while remaining very much an unsettling and frightful monster, is also a figure who embodies the sin of envy. He sees that the warriors feasting and singing in Heorot are enjoying fellowship, while he, Grendel, is lonely and isolated. But rather than responding in a virtuous way to seek out some kind of fellowship for himself, Grendel reacts with hatred. The men of Heorot have what he lacks – so he murders them.

It's a vivid externalization of what envy does to the human heart if left unchecked: it turns to hatred, violence (physical or emotional), to the destruction of fellowship, and, ultimately, to the destruction of one's own soul. Similarly, Grendel's mother can be seen to embody the sin of anger: her natural and understandable grief at her son's death turns outward in violence. And the dragon is a powerful image of greed: sitting on its pile of treasure, which it can neither use nor eat, it nevertheless resents the loss of even one tiny piece – and, once again, this unchecked sin leads to violence, as the dragon unleashes destruction far out of proportion to the theft.

This aspect of the poem resonates strongly with readers of all ages. I have taught this poem to teenagers in their first year at college, and to adult graduate students, but perhaps the encounter that most showed the moral power of *Beowulf* was a conversation I had with my then-five-year-old goddaughter after reading her an illustrated children's version of the tale. We talked about the poem and how Grendel had been jealous of the people in Heorot Hall and behaved very badly. She gravely said, "Sometimes I feel like I have a little Grendel inside me." "Sometimes I feel that way too," I said. And then we talked about positive ways to deal with negative emotions, so that we could *not* be like Grendel.

Envy, anger, greed: we all have to recognize, and battle with, our own monsters. In teaching this poem, I have found this theme to be an excellent way to introduce and discuss the concepts of sin and virtue without bringing in explicitly Christian terms, as these often cause non-Christian students to distance themselves from the material, under the assumption that they're going to get a moral lecture.

I found this aspect of the poem equally valuable in teaching Christian students. For one thing, they, too, benefited from a fresh approach to discussions of sin and virtue, not because they would reject the concepts, but because the concepts were all too familiar. Monsters and dragons presented a way to encounter these ideas afresh and not just tune out, assuming that they were going to hear the same old tired moral exhortations as usual. Many of these young people affirmed 'Christian values', while others were rebelling against what they perceived as meaningless, hypocritical restrictions – but in both cases, they usually had little grasp of what sin and virtue might mean in terms of the interior life. *Beowulf* helped to make the interior life visible and thus able to be reflected upon and taken seriously.

SELECTION

Beowulf's fight with Grendel

From *Beowulf,* translated by John Lesslie Hall

From Book II: Scyld's Successors, Hrothgar's Great Mead-Hall

Then glory in battle to Hrothgar was given, . . .
It burned in his spirit
To urge his folk to found a great building,
A mead-hall grander than men of the era
Ever had heard of, and in it to share
With young and old all of the blessings
The Lord had allowed him, save life and retainers. . . .
Heorot he named it
Who wide-reaching word-sway wielded 'mong earlmen.
His promise he brake not, rings he lavished,
Treasure at banquet. Towered the hall up
High and horn-crested, huge between antlers:
It battle-waves bided, the blasting fire-demon;
Ere long then from hottest hatred must sword-wrath
Arise for a woman's husband and father.
Then the mighty war-spirit endured for a season,
Bore it bitterly, he who bided in darkness,
That light-hearted laughter loud in the building
Greeted him daily; there was dulcet harp-music,
Clear song of the singer. He said that was able
To tell from of old earthmen's beginnings,
That Father Almighty earth had created,
The winsome wold that the water encircleth,
Set exultingly the sun's and the moon's beams
To lavish their lustre on land-folk and races,
And earth He embellished in all her regions
With limbs and leaves; life He bestowed too
On all the kindreds that live under heaven.
So blessed with abundance, brimming with joyance,
The warriors abided, till a certain one gan to
Dog them with deeds of direfullest malice,
A foe in the hall-building: this horrible stranger
Was Grendel entitled, the march-stepper famous

He is eager to build a great hall in which he may feast his retainers.

The hall is completed, and is called Heort, or Heorot.

The Monster Grendel is madly envious of the Danemen's joy.

[The course of the story is interrupted by a short reference to some old account of the creation.]

The glee of the warriors is overcast by a horrible dread.

Who dwelt in the moor-fens, the marsh and the fastness;
The wan-mooded being abode for a season
In the land of the giants, when the Lord and Creator
Had banned him and branded. For that bitter murder,
The killing of Abel, all-ruling Father
The kindred of Cain crushed with His vengeance;
In the feud He rejoiced not, but far away drove him
From kindred and kind, that crime to atone for,
Meter of Justice. Thence ill-favored creatures,
Elves and giants, monsters of ocean,
Came into being, and the giants that longtime
Grappled with God; He gave them requital.

Cain is referred to as a progenitor of Grendel, and of monsters in general.

From Book III: Grendel the Murderer

When the sun was sunken, [Grendel] set out to visit
The lofty hall-building, how the Ring-Danes
had used it
For beds and benches when the banquet was over.
Then he found there reposing many a noble
Asleep after supper; sorrow the heroes,
Misery knew not. The monster of evil
Greedy and cruel tarried but little,
Fell and frantic, and forced from their slumbers
Thirty of thanemen; thence he departed
Leaping and laughing, his lair to return to,
With surfeit of slaughter sallying homeward.
In the dusk of the dawning, as the day was just breaking,
Was Grendel's prowess revealed to the warriors:
Then, his meal-taking finished, a moan was uplifted,
Morning-cry mighty. The man-ruler famous,
The long-worthy atheling, sat very woful,
Suffered great sorrow, sighed for his liegemen,
When they had seen the track of the hateful pursuer,
The spirit accursèd: too crushing that sorrow,
Too loathsome and lasting. Not longer he tarried,
But one night after continued his slaughter
Shameless and shocking, shrinking but little
From malice and murder; they mastered him fully. . . .
So ruled he and strongly strove against justice
Lone against all men, till empty uptowered
The choicest of houses. Long was the season:
Twelve-winters' time torture suffered
The friend of the Scyldings, every affliction.

Grendel attacks the sleeping heroes

He drags off thirty of them, and devours them

A cry of agony goes up, when Grendel's horrible deed is fully realized.

The monster returns the next night.

King Hrothgar's agony and suspense last twelve years.

From Book VII: Hrothgar and Beowulf

"Hail thou, Hrothgar! I am Higelac's kinsman
And vassal forsooth; many a wonder
I dared as a stripling. The doings of Grendel,
In far-off fatherland I fully did know of:
Sea-farers tell us, this hall-building standeth,
Excellent edifice, empty and useless
To all the earlmen after evenlight's glimmer
'Neath heaven's bright hues hath hidden its glory.
This my earls then urged me, the most excellent of them,
Carles very clever, to come and assist thee,
Folk-leader Hrothgar; fully they knew of
The strength of my body. . . . alone now with Grendel
I shall manage the matter, with the monster of evil,
The giant, decide it. Thee I would therefore
Beg of thy bounty, Bright-Danish chieftain,
Lord of the Scyldings, this single petition:
Not to refuse me, defender of warriors,
Friend-lord of folks, so far have I sought thee,
That I may unaided, my earlmen assisting me,
This brave-mooded war-band, purify Heorot.
I have heard on inquiry, the horrible creature
From veriest rashness recks not for weapons;
I this do scorn then, so be Higelac gracious,
My liegelord belovèd, lenient of spirit,
To bear a blade or a broad-fashioned target,
A shield to the onset; only with hand-grip
The foe I must grapple, fight for my life then,
Foeman with foeman; he fain must rely on
The doom of the Lord whom death layeth hold of.
I ween he will wish, if he win in the struggle,
To eat in the war-hall earls of the Geat-folk,
Boldly to swallow them, as of yore he did often
The best of the Hrethmen! Thou needest not trouble
A head-watch to give me; he will have me dripping
And dreary with gore, if death overtake me,
Will bear me off bleeding, biting and mouthing me,
The hermit will eat me, heedless of pity,
Marking the moor-fens; no more wilt thou need then
Find me my food. If I fall in the battle,
Send to Higelac the armor that serveth
To shield my bosom, the best of equipments,
Richest of ring-mails; 'tis the relic of Hrethla,
The work of Wayland. Goes Weird [Fate] as she must go!"

Beowulf salutes Hrothgar, and then proceeds to boast of his youthful achievements.

He intends to fight Grendel unaided.

Since the monster uses no weapons,

I, too, shall disdain to use any.

Should he crush me, he will eat my companions as he has eaten thy thanes.

In case of my defeat, thou wilt not have the trouble of burying me.

Should I fall, send my armor to my lord, King Higelac.

Weird [Fate] is supreme.

From Book XII: Grendel and Beowulf

'Neath the cloudy cliffs came from the moor then
Grendel going, God's anger bare he.
The monster intended some one of earthmen
In the hall-building grand to entrap and make way with:
He went under welkin where well he knew of
The wine-joyous building, brilliant with plating,
Gold-hall of earthmen. Not the earliest occasion
He the home and manor of Hrothgar had sought:
Ne'er found he in life-days later nor earlier
Hardier hero, hall-thanes more sturdy!
Then came to the building the warrior marching,
Bereft of his joyance. The door quickly opened
On fire-hinges fastened, when his fingers had touched it;
The fell one had flung then – his fury so bitter –
Open the entrance. Early thereafter
The foeman trod the shining hall-pavement,
Strode he angrily; from the eyes of him glimmered
A lustre unlovely likest to fire.
He beheld in the hall the heroes in numbers,
A circle of kinsmen sleeping together,
A throng of thanemen: then his thoughts were exultant,
He minded to sunder from each of the thanemen
The life from his body, horrible demon,
Ere morning came, since fate had allowed him
The prospect of plenty. Providence willed not
To permit him any more of men under heaven
To eat in the night-time. Higelac's kinsman
Great sorrow endured how the dire-mooded creature
In unlooked-for assaults were likely to bear him.
No thought had the monster of deferring the matter,
But on earliest occasion he quickly laid hold of
A soldier asleep, suddenly tore him,
Bit his bone-prison, the blood drank in currents,
Swallowed in mouthfuls: he soon had the dead man's
Feet and hands, too, eaten entirely.
Nearer he strode then, the stout-hearted warrior
Snatched as he slumbered, seizing with hand-grip,
Forward the foeman foined with his hand;
Caught he quickly the cunning deviser,
On his elbow he rested. This early discovered
The master of malice, that in middle-earth's regions,
'Neath the whole of the heavens, no hand-grapple greater
In any man else had he ever encountered:

Grendel comes from the fens.

He goes towards the joyous building

This was not his first visit there.

His horrid fingers tear the door open.

He strides furiously into the hall.

He exults over his supposed prey.

Fate has decreed that he shall devour no more heroes. Beowulf suffers from suspense.

Grendel immediately seizes a sleeping warrior, and devours him.

Beowulf and Grendel grapple.

The monster is amazed at Beowulf's strength.

Fearful in spirit, faint-mooded waxed he,
Not off could betake him; death he was pondering,
Would fly to his covert, seek the devils' assembly:
His calling no more was the same he had followed
Long in his lifetime. The liege-kinsman worthy
Of Higelac minded his speech of the evening,
Stood he up straight and stoutly did seize him.
His fingers crackled; the giant was outward,
The earl stepped farther. The famous one minded
To flee away farther, if he found an occasion,
And off and away, avoiding delay,
To fly to the fen-moors; he fully was ware of
The strength of his grapple in the grip of the foeman.

He is anxious to flee.

Beowulf recalls his boast of the evening, and determines to fulfil it.

From Book XIII: Grendel Is Vanquished

For no cause whatever would the earlmen's defender
Leave in life-joys the loathsome newcomer,
He deemed his existence utterly useless
To men under heaven. . . .
But Higelac's hardy henchman and kinsman
Held him by the hand; hateful to other
Was each one if living. A body-wound suffered
The direful demon, damage incurable
Was seen on his shoulder, his sinews were shivered,
His body did burst. To Beowulf was given
Glory in battle; Grendel from thenceward
Must flee and hide him in the fen-cliffs and marshes,
Sick unto death, his dwelling must look for
Unwinsome and woful; he wist the more fully
The end of his earthly existence was nearing,
His life-days' limits. At last for the Danemen,
When the slaughter was over, their wish was accomplished.
The comer-from-far-land had cleansed then of evil,
Wise and valiant, the war-hall of Hrothgar,
Saved it from violence. He joyed in the night-work,
In repute for prowess; the prince of the Geatmen
For the East-Danish people his boast had accomplished,
Bettered their burdensome bale-sorrows fully,
The craft-begot evil they erstwhile had suffered
And were forced to endure from crushing oppression,
Their manifold misery. 'Twas a manifest token,
When the hero-in-battle the hand suspended,
The arm and the shoulder (there was all of the claw
Of Grendel together) 'neath great-stretching hall-roof.

Beowulf has no idea of letting Grendel live.

Grendel is sorely wounded.

His body bursts.

The monster flees away to hide in the moors.

Beowulf suspends Grendel's hand and arm in Heorot.

From Book XXVI: Hrothgar Moralizes – Rest after Labor

Hrothgar advises Beowulf:

"Oh, Beowulf dear,
Best of the heroes, from bale-strife defend thee,
And choose thee the better, counsels eternal;
Beware of arrogance, world-famous champion!
But a little-while lasts thy life-vigor's fulness;
'Twill after hap early, that illness or sword-edge
Shall part thee from strength, or the grasp of the fire,
Or the wave of the current, or clutch of the edges,
Or flight of the war-spear, or age with its horrors,
Or thine eyes' bright flashing shall fade into darkness:
'Twill happen full early, excellent hero,
That death shall subdue thee."

Be not over proud: life is fleeting, and its strength soon wasteth away.

RECOMMENDED RESOURCES

For *Beowulf*, there are many good options for a translation; in fact, there are so many translations that the choice can be a bit overwhelming.

Seamus Heaney, *Beowulf: A New Verse Translation*. This is my preferred version. Heaney, a gifted poet, brings *Beowulf* to life with what I find to be a satisfactory balance between accuracy and freshness of translation. There is a paperback edition with the Old English original on facing pages, as well as an illustrated edition (with John Niles). Heaney's translation is also used in the Norton Critical Edition of *Beowulf*, which includes valuable supporting essays and contextual materials for more advanced (college-level) study of the poem. If you are looking for a one-volume edition for more advanced students, this would be the best choice.

Michael Alexander, *The First Poems in English* (Penguin Classics). This anthology includes a concise rendition of *Beowulf*, with summaries of sections followed by extracts in poetic translation.

Kevin Crossley-Holland, *The Anglo-Saxon World* (Oxford World's Classics). The merit of this edition is its convenience, as it includes an excellent selection of other poetry (including the ones discussed in this book) and prose. However, the translation of *Beowulf* is a bit dull, so if you plan to do more than dip into it, I encourage you to get Heaney's translation.

John Lesslie Hall, *Beowulf: An Anglo-Saxon Epic Poem*. This older translation (1892) is one of the best versions available in the public domain; it includes a glossary and has a useful running annotation on the poem. It is available at Project Gutenberg (https://gutenberg.org/files/16328/16328-h/16328-h.htm).

J.R.R. Tolkien, *Beowulf*. This is a prose translation, focused on linguistic accuracy; Tolkien didn't write it for publication, but rather used it as a teaching aid for his Old English lectures at Oxford. It wouldn't be my first choice as a main text, but it's a solid supporting resource for understanding the poem.

Michael Morpugo, *Beowulf*, illustrated by Michael Foreman. This is a retelling, not a translation, aimed at younger readers. It is excellent, and I highly recommend it.

Gareth Hinds, *Beowulf*. This is a graphic novel adaptation of the poem, and is also worthwhile.

QUESTIONS FOR DISCUSSION

1. Grendel is enraged by the joy of the celebrations in Heorot Hall, and particularly by the song about God's creation of the earth. What is the spiritual significance of this?

2. After Beowulf defeats Grendel, he confronts Grendel's mother. In what way does she embody the sin of anger, as opposed to righteous anger? She is sometimes assumed to be the only female figure in the poem, but we also see Queen Wealhtheow, though she has only a small part in the poem. What role does Wealhtheow play in the story?

3. One of Hrothgar's warriors, Unferth, is at first hostile to Beowulf, accusing Beowulf of boastfulness and overconfidence. Later, however, Unferth shows a change of heart by lending his sword to Beowulf for the fight with Grendel's mother. Discuss Unferth's spiritual challenges and growth.

4. Is Hrothgar's advice to Beowulf relevant for the modern day? Why or why not?

5. In modern retellings or adaptations of stories, it is increasingly common for the villain or monster to be rehabilitated as merely misunderstood, or as the victim or even hero of the story. What is the value of this type of reversal? What is the danger of it? How is the moral framework of *Beowulf* changed if the monsters are misunderstood, not malicious?

6. Compare Beowulf's decision to fight Grendel unarmed with his decision to attack the dragon without the aid of his retainers. Does Beowulf show a moral failing in his decision to face the dragon alone? Why or why not?

7. In what ways is Beowulf a Christ-figure?

8. The *Beowulf*-poet sets his poem in a pre-Christian past and in a different country (not in contemporary Britain). Why do you think he does this? What is the effect?

9. Bullying, racism, sexism, and other forms of marginalization and oppression usually involve treating a person as "other" – less than fully human – rather than as having equal human dignity. Both Grendel and Grendel's mother are human-like, but monstrous. Do these characters encourage a dehumanizing attitude? In what ways can we read *Beowulf* to avoid falling into that attitude?

USING THE ARTS

1. Compare the artistic representations of the characters (Beowulf, Grendel, etc.) in illustrated versions of the poem to the descriptions in the poem. What has the illustrator chosen to emphasize? How does this shape our understanding of the story?

2. Draw a creature to correspond with each of the seven deadly sins. Draw a creature to correspond with the seven lively virtues. Discuss.

3. Have participants create dramatic skits of scenes from the poem. For more advanced groups, consider having them adapt the scene to take place in the modern day.

Elegies

The three poems in this section all come from the Exeter Book, a tenth-century manuscript – one of only four surviving collections of Old English poetry. "The Seafarer," "The Ruin," and "The Wife's Lament" are part of the literary genre called the *elegy*: lyric poems that express sadness for what has been lost, both cultural and personal.

In these poems, we find many examples of a characteristic literary device used in Old English poetry, called a "kenning." This is a vivid, imaginative compound word or descriptive phrase. It might be metaphorical, or substituting a part for the whole, or it might be colorfully descriptive. Some examples of kennings include "whale-road" or "swan-path" for the sea; "bone-house" for the human body; "Guardian of Heaven" for God; "birds of battle" for crows, which are carrion feeders; "gold-giver" for a king, since a good king gives out wealth to his people; and "feasting-place" for a hall. Sometimes kennings are crafted to meet the need for alliteration in a line. More often, they contain compressed meaning that adds to our appreciation of the material.

"The Seafarer"

One of the most famous of the Old English elegies, "The Seafarer" gives a first-person account of longing and loss. We have a vivid depiction of the narrator's hard life at sea, enduring physical hardship but most of all coming to grips with the loneliness of exile. The poet-narrator moves from his recollection of his own experiences to a meditation on the transience of earthly life and the importance of orienting one's life to God.

The narrator is conveying a fundamental truth of the Christian life – the need to recognize that our earthly life is short, and that we must face a reckoning at death – but does so in a way that doesn't feel preachy. In part, the poet achieves this through the masterful use of imagery. The first part of the poem is filled with vibrant images of the sea and the natural world. Some anthologies only print this first portion, omitting the second half, which provides the specifically Christian reflection on the theme. It's well worth making the effort to include both parts in a discussion of the poem. The first part presents the longing of the human soul for its true home in a powerfully implicit way: the sailor recalls his sufferings, yet his heart is still filled by a desire to go out again to the sea. The second part of the poem provides, as it were, a commentary on the first part, with a flavor that is reminiscent of the book of Wisdom in the Bible.

"The Ruin"

In "The Ruin," the poet reflects on a civilizational decline: composing this poem in the eighth century, the poet would have been well aware of the decline from the high point of Roman Britain. From Hadrian's Wall to the Roman roads, from the ruins of aqueducts and public baths to fragments of mosaics depicting exotic foods, the relics of a more cultured and technologically adept past were literal features of the landscape.

We can imagine our poet wandering through the ruins of a Roman villa, reflecting not just on the decaying condition of the buildings, but on the more subtle and devastating loss of knowledge represented by those crumbling hypocausts and broken water-pipes. The handiwork of past generations represented technological skill beyond anyone in the present day. The poet paints a vivid picture of an impressive building fallen to pieces, inviting us to reflect on the process of decay and death, and to appreciate the tragedy of a shattered past that cannot readily be rebuilt or recovered. There's a poetic irony in the fact that the text of "The Ruin" is itself incomplete, due to damage to the only manuscript that contains the poem.

Without indulging in excesses of melancholy (the Old English poets were anything but sentimental), "The Ruin" invites us to look squarely at loss and decay, and to face the transience of human endeavor. The poem is a subtle expression of a Christian form of meditation that has slipped out of fashion in the modern era: the *memento mori*, the reminder of our death.

"The Wife's Lament"

While "The Ruin" evokes a sense of loss for a civilization the poet knows only by its rubble, "The Wife's Lament" draws the reader into the immediacy of personal grief and loss. The details of the narrator's circumstances are only hinted at in the poem, but the basic situation is clear: she is in exile, as a feud has separated her from her husband. The poem expresses her own misery, her great love for her husband, her anxiety for his safety, and her profound longing to be reunited with him.

Here, the poet draws on nature imagery to powerfully evoke a sense of loss. She is forced to live in a cavern, an "earth-cave" in a gloomy valley; this is suggestive of death and burial. Just as tangled briars choke the valley, so too she is choked up with grief and longing.

The poem faces directly the universal human experience of loss; neither here nor in "The Ruin" is there a happy ending or an upbeat message. And that's one of the most important aspects of these poems. The Old English poets here invite us to name our griefs and to look at them honestly, and in so doing, to engage with the most fundamental issues of our existence.

SELECTION

"The Seafarer"

Full poem from *Select Translations from Old English Poetry* by Albert S. Cook and Chauncey B. Tinker; translated by Lola LaMotte Iddings.

PART I

I can sing of myself a true song, of my voyages telling,
How oft through laborious days, through the wearisome hours
I have suffered; have borne tribulations; explored in my ship,
'Mid the terrible rolling of waves, habitations of sorrow.
Benumbed by the cold, oft the comfortless night-watch hath held me
At the prow of my craft as it tossed about under the cliffs.
My feet were imprisoned with frost, were fettered with ice-chains,
Yet hotly were wailing the querulous sighs round my heart;
And hunger within me, sea-wearied, made havoc of courage.
This he, whose lot happily chances on land, doth not know;
Nor how I on the ice-cold sea passed the winter in exile,
In wretchedness, robbed of my kinsmen, with icicles hung.
The hail flew in showers about me ; and there I heard only
The roar of the sea, ice-cold waves, and the song of the swan;
For pastime the gannets' cry served me; the kittiwakes' chatter
For laughter of men; and for mead-drink the call of the sea-mews.
When storms on the rocky cliffs beat, then the terns, icy-feathered,
Made answer; full oft the sea-eagle forebodingly screamed,
The eagle with pinions wave-wet. There none of my kinsmen
Might gladden my desolate soul; of this little he knows
Who possesses the pleasures of life, who has felt in the city
Some hardship, some trifling adversity, proud and wine-flushed.
How weary I oft had to tarry upon the sea-way!
The shadows of night became darker, it snowed from the north;
The world was enchained by the frost; hail fell upon earth;
'Twas the coldest of grain. Yet the thoughts of my heart now
are throbbing

To test the high streams, the salt waves in tumultuous play.
Desire in my heart ever urges my spirit to wander
To seek out the home of the stranger in lands afar off.
There is no one that dwells upon earth, so exalted in mind,
So large in his bounty, nor yet of such vigorous youth,
Nor so daring in deeds, nor to whom his liege lord is so kind,
But that he has always a longing, a sea-faring passion
For what the Lord God shall bestow, be it honor or death.
No heart for the harp has he, nor for acceptance of treasure,
No pleasure has he in a wife, no delight in the world,
Nor in aught save the roll of the billows; but always a longing,
A yearning uneasiness, hastens him on to the sea.
The woodlands are captured by blossoms, the hamlets grow fair,
Broad meadows are beautiful, earth again bursts into life,
And all stir the heart of the wanderer eager to journey,
So he meditates going afar on the pathway of tides.
The cuckoo, moreover, gives warning with sorrowful note,
Summer's harbinger sings, and forebodes to the heart bitter sorrow.
The nobleman comprehends not, the luxurious man,
What some must endure, who travel the farthest in exile.
Now my spirit uneasily turns in the heart's narrow chamber,
Now wanders forth over the tide, o'er the home of the whale,
To the ends of the earth – and comes back to me. Eager and greedy,
The lone wanderer screams, and resistlessly drives my soul onward,
Over the whale-path, over the tracts of the sea.

PART II

The delights of the Lord are far dearer to me than this dead,
Fleeting life upon earth, for I can not believe that earth's riches
For ever endure. Each one of three things, ere its time comes,
Is always uncertain: violence, age, and disease
Wrench the soul away, doomed to depart. This is praise from the living,
From those who speak afterwards, this the best fame after death –
That ere he departed he labored, and wrought daring deeds
'Gainst the malice of fiends, and the devil; so men shall extol him,
His praise among angels shall live, ever, world without end,
His the blessing of life everlasting, and joy 'mid the hosts.
The days have departed, all pomps of earth's kingdom have vanished;

There now are no kings, no emperors now, no gold-givers
As of yore, when they wrought in their midst the most glorious deeds,
And lived in the lordliest power. This glory has fallen,
Delights have all vanished away; the weak ones remain,
And these govern the world, obtaining their pleasure with effort.
Power has declined, earth's glory grows aged and sear,
Like every man now in the world; old age overtakes him,
His countenance loses its color, gray-haired he laments;
He has seen his old friends, sons of princes, consigned to the earth.
This garment of flesh has no power, when the spirit escapes,
To drink in the sweet nor to taste of the bitter; it then
Has no power to stretch forth the hands or to think with the mind.
Though the grave should be covered with gold by the nearest of kin,
Be buried along with the dead in masses of treasure,
Still that will not go with them. Gold can no substitute be
For the fear of the Lord, to the soul which is laden with sin,
Which aforetime, so long as it lived, kept that treasure concealed.
Great is the fear of the Lord; the earth trembles before it;
He established the unmovable earth, the world and the heavens.
Foolish is he who stands not in awe of the Lord –
Unexpectedly death comes upon him; but happy is he
Who lives humble in mind, to him cometh honor from heaven;
God doth establish the soul that believes in His might.
One should check a strong will, and should govern it firmly,
Be true unto men, and be clean in his manner of life. . . .
Fate, God the Creator, is stronger than any man's will.
Come, let us reflect where our home is, consider the way
By which we go thither; then let us each strive to press forward
To joy everlasting, where life has its source in God's love,
Where is heavenly hope. Then to Him who is holy be thanks,
Because He hath honored us; thanks to the Ruler of Heaven,
The Lord everlasting, throughout all the ages! Amen.

SELECTION

"The Ruin"

Translation adapted from *Anglo-Saxon and Norse Poems*,
edited and translated by Nora Kershaw

Wondrous is this masonry, broken by the Fates;
the fortifications have given way, the buildings raised by giants
are crumbling.
The roofs have collapsed, the towers are in ruins,
The gates are broken, there is hoarfrost on the mortar,
The walls are rent and broken away, and have fallen,
undermined by age. The owners and builders are perished and gone,
held fast in the earth's embrace, the ruthless clutch of the grave,
while a hundred generations of mankind have passed away.
Red of hue and hoary with lichen, this wall has outlasted kingdom
after kingdom,
remained standing under storms. The lofty arch has fallen.

. . . .

Resolute in spirit he marvellously clamped the foundation of the
walls with wire ties.
There were splendid palaces, and many halls with water flowing
through them;
a wealth of gables towered aloft. Loud was the clamour of the troops;
many were the mead-halls, full of the joys of life,
until all was shattered by mighty Fate.
The dead lay on all sides. Days of pestilence had come,
and all the warriors were carried off by death.
Their defences became waste places, their fortifications crumbled;
the troops who should have repaired them lay dead on the earth.
And so these courts lie desolate, and the framework of the dome
with its red arches sheds its tiles. . . .
where of old many a warrior, joyous hearted and radiant with gold,
shone resplendent in the harness of battle, proud and flushed with wine.

He gazed upon the treasure, the silver, the precious stones,
upon wealth, riches and pearls, upon this splendid citadel of a broad
domain.
There stood courts of stone, and a stream gushed forth in rippling
floods of hot water.
The wall enfolded within its bright bosom the whole place
which contained the hot flood of the baths. That was convenient.
Then they let pour hot streams over gray stone.
. . . .

SELECTION

"The Wife's Lament"

From *Old English Poems Translated into the Original Meter*, edited by Cosette Faust and Stith Thompson

Sorrowfully I sing my song of woe,
My tale of trials. In truth I may say
That the buffets I have borne since my birth in the world
Were never more than now, either new or old.
Ever the evils of exile I endure!
Long since went my lord from the land of his birth,
Over the welling waves. Woeful at dawn I asked
Where lingers my lord, in what land does he dwell?
Then I fared into far lands and faithfully sought him,
A weary wanderer in want of comfort.
His treacherous tribesmen contrived a plot,
Dark and dastardly, to drive us apart
The width of a world, where with weary hearts
We live in loneliness, and longing consumes me.
My master commanded me to make my home here.
Alas, in this land my loved ones are few,
My faithful friends! Hence I feel great sorrow
That the man well-matched with me I have found
To be sad in soul and sorrowful in mind,
Concealing his thoughts and thinking of murder,
Though blithe in his bearing. Oft we bound us by oath
That the day of our death should draw us apart,
Nothing less end our love. Alas, all is changed!
Now is as naught, as if never it were,
Our faith and our friendship. Far and near I shall
Endure the hate of one dear to my heart!
He condemned me to dwell in a darksome wood,
Under an oak-tree in an earth-cave drear.

Old is the earth-hall. I am anxious with longing.
Dim are the dales, dark the hills tower,
Bleak the tribe-dwellings, with briars entangled,
Unblessed abodes. Here bitterly I have suffered
The faring of my lord afar. Friends there are on earth
Living in love, in lasting bliss,
While, wakeful at dawn, I wander alone
Under the oak-tree the earth-cave near.
Sadly I sit there the summer-long day,
Wearily weeping my woeful exile,
My many miseries. Hence I may not ever
Cease my sorrowing, my sad bewailing,
Nor all the longings of my life of woe.
Always may the young man be mournful of spirit,
Unhappy of heart, and have as his portion
Many sorrows of soul, unceasing breast-cares,
Though now blithe of behavior. Unbearable likewise
Be his joys in the world. Wide be his exile
To far-away folk-lands where my friend sits alone,
A stranger under stone-cliffs, by storm made hoary,
A weary-souled wanderer, by waters encompassed,
In his lonely lodging. My lover endures
Unmeasured mind-care: he remembers too oft
A happier home. To him is fate cruel
Who lingers and longs for the loved one's return!

RECOMMENDED RESOURCES

Kevin Crossley-Holland, translator and editor, *The Anglo-Saxon World: An Anthology* (Oxford World's Classics). As I noted for "The Dream of the Rood," this volume is my first choice as a text for general reading and with students. It contains all three elegies discussed here, but oddly, the translation of "The Seafarer" included here omits the last few lines of Christian exhortation.

Richard Hamer, editor, *A Choice of Anglo-Saxon Verse*, revised and expanded edition (Faber, 2015). This volume offers a generous selection of poems in excellent translations with the original Old English reproduced on facing pages. All three of the elegies discussed here are included, and "The Seafarer" is presented in full. The introductory material is briefer than in Crossley-Holland's volume, however.

S.A.J. Bradley, translator and editor, *Anglo-Saxon Poetry* (Everyman). This volume provides prose translations of a large selection of Old English poems, including all three of the elegies discussed here (and with a full rendering of "The Seafarer"). Though using prose, Bradley keeps a poetic quality to the translations, making this a useful resource.

QUESTIONS FOR DISCUSSION

1. What is the difference between lamentation and complaining? What are the results of each?

2. Consider how "The Seafarer" and "The Wife's Lament" express longing. Have you ever experienced a sense of longing or dissatisfaction with the world? How can we relate this feeling to our life as Christians?

3. What aspects of our modern culture shape us to expect constant "progress"? What does "The Ruin" challenge about this assumption?

4. The book of Psalms contains many laments, both individual and communal (such as Psalms 55, 88, and 90). What is the effect of praying through a text that expresses grief and loss if you are not, personally, feeling that way? Or if you are?

5. Many Christians are afraid of expressing doubt or acknowledging suffering. How does this affect our evangelization and discipleship efforts?

6. Anxiety and depression are issues that are often avoided, feared, or glossed over by Christians. The result is that those who suffer are often marginalized or ignored. How can we use imaginative strategies for better pastoral care?

USING THE ARTS

1. The Church year includes times specifically for lament, most notably Lent (and specifically Ash Wednesday and Good Friday) and Advent; Fridays are also penitential days, as corresponding with the death of Christ on a Friday. Create an artistic scene of a landscape (with or without buildings) that evokes the meaning of one of these seasons. Discuss.

2. Write an elegy, using "The Ruin," "The Seafarer," or "The Wife's Lament" as a model.

Christ I

The Exeter Book manuscript, where we find the moving elegies that we have just discussed, also contains the long poem *Christ*, attributed to Cynewulf, one of the few Old English poets whose name has come down to us. The poem has three distinct parts, each with a different theme and drawing on different source material: *Christ I* deals with Advent, *Christ II* with the Ascension, and *Christ III* with the Second Coming.

For this volume, I've chosen to focus on *Christ I*, as its Advent theme links up in an intriguing way with our present-day Catholic liturgy and devotional practices. As a fellow Catholic with a thousand years of difference in perspective, Cynewulf can help us to gain a fresh perspective on matters of our faith that may have become stale through overfamiliarity.

The liturgical season of Advent, comprising the four Sundays and following days leading up to December 25, has unfortunately become rather overshadowed by the lead-up to Christmas in popular culture, and has lost much of its penitential quality. Since Advent calls us to reflect on both the first coming of Christ in history and the Second Coming of Christ in judgment, the traditional themes of this pre-Christmas season are the four last things (death, judgment, heaven, and hell).

These themes are, to say the least, not in the 'Christmas spirit' as understood in the wider culture, with its relentless emphasis on jollity (whether you feel like it or not), family togetherness (assuming you have one), and above all, shopping for gifts (with the toxic association of spending money with expressing love). It can be a remarkably stressful and depressing season, and Christmas Day itself can feel like an emotional letdown after two months of buildup. Then, in this modern version of Christmas, the days following December 25 are dull and empty. The holiday is over, and people take down the decorations . . . but this is exactly the opposite of what it should be.

After a sober and reflective Advent season, the twelve days of Christmas *begin* (not end) with December 25, so that the season of festivity runs to January 6, the Epiphany, when Christ is made known to the Gentiles, represented by the Magi. An older tradition continues the festal tone all the way through February 2, Candlemas, which marks the presentation of the newborn Jesus at the temple.

While all the world is shopping and having Christmas parties, we ought to be meditating on our need for a Savior; when all the world is exhausted and stuck in the gloom of gray January, we ought to be in full celebratory swing!

Here we find our connection with *Christ I*, for it provides an opportunity to enter into the Advent devotional season through the Great O Antiphons. You might not have heard them referred to by that name, but the great Advent hymn 'O Come Emmanuel' is based on these images. The Great O Antiphons originated in the early medieval period in Italy; in fact, there is an allusion to "O Sapientia" in Boethius's *The Consolation of Philosophy*, which was written around the year 524. They soon inspired devotional poetry in the vernacular languages, including *Christ I*, our text in this section.

An antiphon is a short prayer that is sung or said before another reading in the liturgy, thematically related to the text or to the season. The "O Antiphons" are used in the liturgy on the last seven days of Advent; they take their name from the direct address of each to our Lord under a different title: O Sapientia (Wisdom), O Adonai (Lord), O Radix Jesse (Root of Jesse), O Clavis (Key), O Oriens (Light), O Rex Gentium (King of the Nations), and O Emmanuel (God-with-us). The first letter of each spells, in reverse, the Latin phrase *Ero Cras*, which means "Tomorrow, I will come."

The poem we call *Christ I* is in fact a set of twelve separate lyric poems, rather than one extended poem; each lyric focuses on a different Advent image or theme. Since the individual poems are relatively short and stand on their own, they make excellent texts for discussion and devotional activities.

I've chosen here to highlight two of the lyrics in this poem.

Lyric I (of which, sadly, the opening and closing lines are lost) draws on "O Rex Gentium." Here we have an intriguing blending of images. It begins with Christ as the cornerstone, developing into an extended metaphor of Christ as the foundation for a royal hall – which has now fallen into decay. At the end, the poem shifts the image of the building into that of the Body of Christ. The image of Christ as King, then, shows him as simultaneously the master builder, the cornerstone of the house itself, and its repairer.

Lyric VII, though it is not directly based on one of the Great O Antiphons, strikingly dramatizes the brief passage in Matthew's Gospel when Mary's pregnancy became known, and "her husband Joseph, being a righteous man and unwilling to expose her to public disgrace, planned to dismiss her quietly" (Matt. 1:19). It is one of the earliest examples of the style of dramatic religious dialogue that would become a staple of medieval English sacred drama. What did St. Joseph feel in the time between his discovery of Mary's pregnancy and the revelation by the angel in his dream that this child is of the Holy Spirit?

It is precisely this that Lyric VII addresses, in the form of a conversation between Joseph and Mary. In the poem, Joseph laments the insults and scorn he has received on her account, and he struggles to know what to do. Mary, quietly confident, then reveals the nature of the virginal conception of her Son and invites Joseph to give thanks that he will be known as the earthly father of the Redeemer. It is a moving scene, reminding us of the real humanity of both St. Joseph and Our Lady.

In both of these lyrics, we find a down-to-earth quality that invites reflection on the reality of the Incarnation, and an opportunity to change our perspective about how we approach the Advent season.

SELECTION

Excerpts from *Christ I*

From *Old English Poems Translated into the Original Meter*, edited by Cosette Faust and Stith Thompson

LYRIC I

. . . . to the King.
Thou art the wall-stone that the workmen of old
Rejected from the work. Well it befits thee
To become the head of the kingly hall,
To join in one the giant walls
In thy fast embrace, the flint unbroken;
That through all the earth every eye may see
And marvel evermore, O mighty Prince,
Declare thy accomplishments through the craft of thy hand,
Truth-fast, triumphant, and untorn from its place
Leave wall against wall. For the work it is needful
That the Craftsman should come and the King himself
And raise that roof that lies ruined and decayed,
Fallen from its frame. He formed that body,
The Lord of life, and its limbs of clay,
And shall free from foemen the frightened in heart,
The downcast band, as he did full oft.
. . . .

LYRIC VII

[*Mary*] "O my Joseph, O Jacob's son,
Kinsman of David, the king renowned,
Dost thou plan to turn from thy plighted troth,
And leave my love?"

[*Joseph*] "Alas, full soon
I am oppressed with grief and deprived of honor.
I have borne for thee many bitter words,
Insulting slurs and sorrowful taunts,
Scathing abuses, and they scorn me now
In wrathful tones. My tears I shall pour
In sadness of soul. My sorrowful heart,
My grief full easily our God may heal,
And not leave me forlorn. Alas, young damsel,
Mary maiden!"

[*Mary*] "Why bemoanest thou
And bitterly weepest? No blame in thee,
Nor any fault have I ever found
For wicked works, and this word thou speakest
As if thou thyself with sinful deeds
And faults wert filled."

[*Joseph*] "Far too much grief
Thy conception has caused me to suffer in shame.
How can I bear their bitter taunts
Or ever make answer to my angry foes
Who wish me woe? 'Tis widely known
That I took from the glorious temple of God
A beautiful virgin of virtue unblemished,
The chastest of maidens, but a change has now come,
Though I know not the cause. Nothing avails me –
To speak or to be silent. If I say the truth,
Then the daughter of David shall die for her crime,
Struck down with stones; yet still it were harder
To conceal the sin; forsworn forever
I should live my life loathed by all people,
By men reviled."

Then the maid revealed
The work of wonder, and these words she spoke:

[*Mary*] "Truly I say, by the Son of the Creator
The Savior of souls, the Son of God,
I tell thee in truth that the time has not been
That the embrace of a mortal man I have known
On all the earth; but early in life
This grace was granted me, that Gabriel came,
The high angel of heaven, and hailed me in greeting,
In truthful speech: that the Spirit of heaven
With his light should illumine me, that life's Glory by me
Should be borne, the bright Son, the blessed Child of God,
Of the kingly Creator. I am become now his temple,
Unspoiled and spotless; the Spirit of comfort
Hath his dwelling in me. Endure now no longer
Sorrow and sadness, and say eternal thanks
To the mighty Son of the Maker, that his mother I have become,
Though a maid I remain, and in men's opinion
Thou art famed as his father, if fulfillment should come
Of the truth that the Prophets foretold of his coming."

RECOMMENDED RESOURCES

R.M. Liuzza, *Old English Poetry: An Anthology* (Broadview). This is one of the very few editions that includes a translation of the full text of *Christ I*.

Kevin Crossley-Holland, *The Anglo-Saxon World: An Anthology* (Oxford World's Classics). This edition, which I've noted as very useful overall, includes translations of Lyrics I, II, and VII, titled "Advent Lyrics."

Eleanor Parker has done excellent translations and reflections on many of these poems on her blog, *A Clerk of Oxford*, aclerkofoxford.blogspot.com.

Charles Huntington Whitman, *The Christ of Cynewulf; A Poem in Three Parts: The Advent, The Ascension, and the Last Judgment* (Ginn and Company). This prose translation is a bit stilted but has the significant merit of containing all three parts of "Christ" and of being in the public domain. It can be found here: https://archive.org/details/christcynewulfa00whitgoog/ and also here: http://www.humanitiesweb.org/spa/lcc/ID/778.

Malcolm Guite, *Sounding the Seasons: Seventy Sonnets for the Church Year.* Guite, an Anglican poet, has written a beautiful set of sonnets for the O Antiphons, which are included in this volume. These sonnets are very effective paired with the Old English text.

The modern English text of the Antiphons as used in the Catholic liturgy can be found here: https://www.usccb.org/resources/o-antiphons-advent.

Other notable sections of *Christ I* (not included in the excerpts) are Lyric II, which explores the imagery of "O Clavis," naming Christ as the one who can open the door of our prison house; Lyric VI, which meditates on "O Emmanuel," God-with-us; and Lyric V, which draws on the imagery of "O Oriens." This last will be intriguing to readers of *The Lord of the Rings*, as it was here that J.R.R. Tolkien found the evocative phrase "Ēala ēarendel, engla beorhtast, / ofer middangeard monnum sended" ("Hail Earendel, brightest of angels, / Sent to men over middle-earth"), and from this linguistic inspiration created Eärendil, one of the most significant characters in the mythology of Middle-earth.

QUESTIONS FOR DISCUSSION

1. Do you keep the liturgical season of Advent? If so, how do you express it in your home? In your devotional practices? If not, what might you do to mark this season of the Church year?

2. Lyric I uses the image of Christ as cornerstone. How does this relate to the title of Christ as *Rex Gentium*, the King of all nations?

3. For people in the modern West, and particularly for Americans, the image of Christ as *King* is particularly difficult to engage with. What does the image of "King" suggest to you? What insight can we gain from reflecting on Christ as the true King of all nations?

4. The image of the broken building in Lyric I connects to the theme of reflecting on death, one of the four last things. What is the spiritual value of the practice of *memento mori*, remembering one's death?

4. In Scripture, we never hear St. Joseph speak, but medieval Christians were entirely comfortable with poetry and drama that presented him as a speaking character. What is your reaction to the dialogue in Lyric VII?

5. Lyric VII portrays doubt, dismay, and anxiety in St. Joseph. Discuss. Have you ever felt that, as a Christian, you were not 'allowed' to feel any of these things?

6. What do we see of Mary's personality in Lyric VII? How does this relate to what we know of her from Scripture?

7. For medieval Christians, there was no cultural tension involved in observing Advent: the entire community would be keeping to the penitential disciplines of the season and then entering fully into the celebration of Christmas. In the modern day, however, the Church's rhythm of fasting and feasting is often entirely at odds with the secular rhythm. How does this mismatch affect our spiritual lives?

8. What opportunities for evangelization are provided by the traditions of Advent?

USING THE ARTS

1. Lyric VII is an early example of what would become the medieval "mystery plays": short dramas depicting scenes in the life of Christ. This poem can be acted out by a pair of students, leading to further discussion about the characters and situation. For a more extended activity, have students write dialogues between other biblical characters, and act them out.

2. Draw illustrations for each of the seven Christ-images in the O Antiphons.

3. Write an expanded version of Lyric I, developing out the poem's missing lines.

4. For musically inclined groups: arrange one or more of the Lyrics as songs.

Pearl

We now move from Old English into Middle English, although it remains necessary to read these texts in translation, since the language is still very different from Modern English.

Here we begin with the gentle poem *Pearl*, which opens with a grief-stricken father visiting the grave of his little daughter, Pearl. The poem is told in the first person and is constructed as a dream vision, just as we saw in "The Dream of the Rood." The narrator, sorrowing, falls asleep on his daughter's grave and has a profound dream. Venturing into a beautiful forest, he encounters a stream, and on the other side, sees his little daughter, alive and well, dressed in white robes. She and her father converse, and she becomes the narrator for the majority of the poem.

Pearl has less of a narrative than "The Dream of the Rood," so it can be helpful for appreciating the poem to have a sense of what the poet is doing ahead of time. Pearl explains that she is in heaven, with Mary the empress and the saints as kings and queens around her – and she, too, is a queen, although she had been only a child when she died, with no accomplishments. This vision prompts her father to ask questions, leading Pearl to tell the parable of the vineyard, followed by further explanations of sin, repentance, and grace. She goes on to explain that she is a Bride of Christ and to give a vivid description of the New Jerusalem. Finally, her father is given a vision of the heavenly city and Christ as the Lamb, and sees his beloved daughter among the procession of maidens in attendance. Although Pearl told him not to try to cross the stream, at this point he attempts to do so, and his disobedience breaks the dream; he awakens, saddened, and reflects on what he has learned.

The dream-vision frame is theologically significant. The full experience of heaven will only occur after the general resurrection on the last day, when all souls will be reunited with their bodies for eternal life (either in heaven or in hell); at this time, all the saved souls will have completed their journey through purgatory. Thus, any glimpses of 'heaven' by souls still tied to their earthly bodies can only be just that: glimpses, visions, hints. It is in fact more accurate, not less, to depict these views of heaven in allegorical and symbolic ways, so as not to confuse people into thinking that this is 'really' what heaven is like (when we do not and cannot know this yet).

What is remarkable about this poem is that it covers such substantial scriptural and theological content, and yet it does so in a way that is remarkably personal and touching. The poet makes deft use of the scene and characters; they are more than a mere framework for the theology. The narrator's questions arise naturally from what he sees; for instance, he cannot understand how his little daughter, who was only two years old when she died, could possibly merit to stand among other kings and queens in heaven. This discussion leads smoothly into a consideration of the riches of God's grace. The allegorical and didactic elements are present throughout the poem, but it always retains the relational thread of the conversation between the loving father and his little daughter, and his grief is handled sympathetically and movingly.

Recognizing that *Pearl* also has an allegorical dimension opens up another level of meaning for the poem. The little girl's name is significant: the pearl is symbolic of purity, and it is also a pointer toward the passages of Scripture that the poet is drawing on here: Matthew 13:45–46: "Again, the kingdom of heaven is like a merchant in search of fine pearls; on finding one pearl of great value, he went and sold all that he had and bought it." Pearl herself brings up this parable! She represents in herself the 'pearl of great price': by connecting this with the very real and powerful love of a father for his daughter, the poet gives us a sense of how we *ought* to love God and strive to enter heaven.

What is perhaps most notable about *Pearl* is the richness and detail of its descriptions. The poet is encouraging us, the readers, to believe the Gospel, to follow Christ, to fix our eyes on heaven, but he doesn't do it through dry abstractions. Rather, he interweaves the theological content with vivid images of the court of heaven, the vineyard in the parable, and the New Jerusalem – all set in the frame of the father and daughter conversing on either side of a lovely stream, inside the further frame of his visiting her grave on a beautiful August day.

Pearl gives us something that is vitally important and that we are by and large missing today: a picture of heaven as beautiful, desirable, real, and something we should be longing for and striving for.

SELECTION

Excerpt from *Pearl*

From Sophie Jewett, *The Pearl, A Middle English Poem: A Modern Version in the Metre of the Original*

Pearl that the Prince full well might prize,
So surely set in shining gold!
No pearl of Orient with her vies;
To prove her peerless I make bold:
So round, so radiant to mine eyes,
smooth she seemed, so small to hold,
Among all jewels judges wise
Would count her best an hundred fold.
Alas! I lost my pearl of old!
I pine with heart-pain unforgot;
Down through my arbour grass it rolled,
My own pearl, precious, without spot.

Since in that spot it slipped from me
I wait, and wish, and oft complain;
Once it would bid my sorrow flee,
And my fair fortune turn again;
It wounds my heart now ceaselessly,
And burns my breast with bitter pain.
Yet never so sweet a song may be
As, this still hour, steals through my brain,
While verity I muse in vain
How clay should her bright beauty clot;
O Earth! a brave gem thou dost stain,
My own pearl, precious, without spot! . . .

Once, to that spot of which I rhyme,
I entered, in the arbour green,
In August, the high summer-time
When corn is cut with sickles keen;

Upon the mound where my pearl fell,
Tall, shadowing herbs grew bright and sheen,
Gilliflower, ginger and gromwell,
With peonies powdered all between.
As it was lovely to be seen,
So sweet the fragrance there, I wot,
Worthy her dwelling who hath been
My own pearl, precious, without spot.

Upon that spot my hands I crossed
In prayer, for cold at my heart caught,
And sudden sorrow surged and tossed,
Though reason reconcilement sought.
I mourned my pearl, dear beyond cost,
And strange fears with my fancy fought;
My will in wretchedness was lost,
And yet Christ comforted my thought.
Such odours to my sense were brought,
I fell upon that flowery plot,
Sleeping, – a sleep with dreams inwrought
Of my pearl, precious, without spot. . . .

For the beauteousness of downs and dales,
Of wood and water and proud plains,
My joy springs up and my grief quails,
My anguish ends, and all my pains.
A swift stream down the valley hales
My feet along. Bliss brims my brains;
The farther I follow those watery vales,
The stronger joy my heart constrains. . . .

There was more of marvel and of grace
Than I could tell, howe'er I tried;
The human heart that could embrace
A tenth part were well satisfied;
For Paradise, the very place,
Must be upon that farther side;
The water by a narrow space
Pleasance from pleasance did divide.
Beyond, on some slope undescried

The City stood, I thought, wherefore
I strove to cross the river's tide,
And ever I longed, yet more and more. . . .

Then a new matter came to hand
That moved my heart yet more and more. . . .

At the cliff's foot a vision stays
My glance, a maiden debonaire,
All glimmering white before my gaze;
And I know her, – have seen her otherwhere.
Like fine gold leaf one cuts with care,
Shone the maiden on the farther shore. . . .

[Pearl:] "Thou rememberest when thy pearl fell low
In earth, I was but young to see;
But my Lord the Lamb, as if to show
His grace, took me His bride to be,
Crowned me a queen in bliss to go
Through length of days eternally;
And dowered with all His wealth is she
Who is His love, and I am His;
His worthiness and royalty
Are root and ground of all my bliss."

"My blissful one, may this be true.
Pardon if I speak ill," I prayed:
"Art thou the queen o' the heaven's blue,
To whom earth's honour shall be paid?
We believe in Mary, of grace who grew,
A mother, yet a blameless maid;
To wear her crown were only due
To one who purer worth displayed." . . .

"Courteous Queen," that bright one said,
And, kneeling, lifted up her face:
"Matchless Mother and merriest Maid,
Blessèd Beginner of every grace."
Then she arose, and softly stayed,
And spoke to me across that space:
"Sir, many seek gain here, and are paid,

But defrauders are none within this place;
That Empress may all heaven embrace,
And earth and hell in her empery;
Her from her heritage none will chase,
For she is Queen of courtesy.

"The court of thc kingdom of God doth thrive
Only because of this wondrous thing:
Each one who therein may arrive,
Of the realm is either queen or king;
And no one the other doth deprive,
But is fain of his fellow's guerdoning,
And would wish each crown might be worth five,
If possible were their bettering.
But my Lady, from whom our Lord did spring,
Rules over all our company,
And for that we all rejoice and sing,
Since she is Queen of courtesy." . . .

[Narrator:] "Courtesy flowers thy folk among,
And charity, I well believe.
If foolish words flow from my tongue,
Let not my speech thy spirit grieve.
A queen in heaven while yet so young,
Too high thou dost thyself upheave.
Then what reward from strife were wrung?
What worship more might he achieve
Who lived in penance morn and eve,
Through bodily pain in bliss to be?
Honour more high might he receive,
Than be crowned king by courtesy?

"That courtesy rewards no deed
If all be true that thou dost say;
Our life not two years didst thou lead
Nor learned to please God, nor to pray,
No Paternoster knew nor creed,
And made a queen on the first day!
I may not think, so God me speed!
That God from right would swerve away;

As a countess, damsel, by my fay!
To live in heaven were a fair boon,
Or like a lady of less array,
But a queen! Ah, no! it is too soon."

"With Him there is no soon nor late,"
Replied to me that worthy wight;
"True always is His high mandate;
He doth no evil, day nor night.
Hear Matthew in the mass narrate,
In the Gospel of the God of might,
His parable portrays the state
Of the Kingdom of Heaven, clear as light:
'My servants,' saith He, 'I requite
As a lord who will his vineyard prune;
The season of the year is right,
And labourers must be hired soon.'

"Right soon the hirelings all may see
How the master with the dawn arose;
To hire his labourers forth went he,
And workmen stout and strong he chose.
For a penny a day they all agree,
Even as the master doth propose,
They toil and travail lustily,
Prune, bind, and with a ditch enclose.
Then to the market-place he goes,
And finds men idle at high noon:
'How can a man stand here who knows
The vineyards should be tilled so soon?'

"'Soon as day dawned we hither won,
And no man hath our labour sought;
We have been standing since rose the sun
And no one bids us to do aught.'
'Enter my vineyard every one,'
The master answered quick as thought:
'The work that each by night has done
I will truly pay, withholding naught.'
Among the vines they went and wrought,

While morning, noon and afternoon,
More labourers the master brought,
Until the night must gather soon.

"Soon fell the time of evensong.
An hour before the sun was set,
He saw more idlers, young and strong;
His voice was sober with regret:
'Why stand ye idle all day long?'
'No man,' they said, 'hath hired us yet.'
'Go to my vineyard, fear no wrong;
Each man an honest wage shall get.'
The day grew dark and darker yet,
Before the rising of the moon;
The master who would pay his debt,
Bade summon all the hirelings soon.

"The lord soon called his steward: 'Go
Bring in the men quick as ye may;
Give them the wages that I owe,
And, lest they aught against me say,
Range them along here in a row,
To each alike his penny pay;
Start with the last who standeth low,
And to the first proceed straightway,'
And then the first began to pray,
Complaining they had travailed sore:
'These wrought but one hour of the day,
We think we should receive the more.'

"'More have we served,' they muttered low,
'Who have endured the long day's heat,
Than these who not two hours toiled so;
Why should their claim with ours compete?'
Said the master: 'I pay all I owe;
Friend, no injustice shalt thou meet;
Take that which is thine own and go.
For a penny we settled in the street;
Why dost thou now for more entreat?
Thou wast well satisfied before.

Once made, a bargain is complete;
Why shouldst thou, threatening, ask for more?

"'What can be more within my gift
Than what I will with mine to do?
Let not thine eyes to evil shift,
Because I trusty am, and true.'
'Thus I,' said Christ, 'all men shall sift.
The last shall be the first of you;
And the first last, however swift,
For many are called, but chosen, few.'
And thus poor men may have their due,
That late and little burden bore;
Their work may vanish like the dew,
The mercy of God is much the more.

"More gladness have I, herewithin,
Of flower of life, and noble name,
Than all men in the world might win,
Who thought their righteous deeds to name.
Nathless even now did I begin;
To the vineyard as night fell I came,
But my Lord would not account it sin;
He paid my wages without blame.
Yet others did not fare the same,
Who toiled and travailed there before,
And of their hire might nothing claim,
Perchance shall not for a year more." . . .

"Flawless maid so mild and meek,"
Then said I to that lovely flower:
"Let me that stately city [the New Jerusalem] seek,
And let me see thy blissful bower."
That bright one said, "Thou art too weak,
Thou may'st not enter to its tower;
Yet of the Lamb I did bespeak
This goodly gift, that He would dower
Thine eyes with the sight for one short hour, –
From without, – within none ever saw;

To step in that street thou hast no power,
Unless thy soul were free from flaw.

"This flawless sight I will not hide;
Up toward the brook's head thou must go,
While I will follow on this side,
Till yonder hill the city show."
And then I would no longer bide,
But stole through branches, bending low,
Till from the summit I espied,
Through green boughs swaying to and fro,
Afar, the city, all aglow,
That brighter than bright sunbeams shone.
In writing it is pictured so,
In the Revelation of St. John. . . .

Of sun or moon they had no need;
For God Himself was their lamp light,
The Lamb their lantern was indeed;
From Him the city shone all bright.
Through wall and dwelling my looks might speed,
Such clearness could not hinder sight.
Of the high throne ye might take heed,
With draperies of radiant white,
As John the Apostle doth endite;
High God Himself did sit thereon.
From the throne a river welled outright
Was brighter than both sun and moon. . . .

Beneath the moon full well might fail
The heart of mortal to endure
The marvel that did mine eyes assail,
Fashioned the fancy to allure.
I stood as still as a startled quail,
For wonder of its fair figure,
I felt no rest and no travail,
Ravished before such radiance pure.
I say, and with conviction sure,
Had the eyes of man received that boon,

Though wisest clerks sought for his cure,
His life were lost beneath the moon.

Now, even as the full moon might rise
Ere daylight doth to darkness fall,
Sudden I saw with still surprise
Within that shining city-wall,
The streets full-thronged in wondrous wise,
Silent, with never a herald's call,
With virgins in the selfsame guise
As my beloved, sweet and small.
Each head was crowned with coronal,
Pearl-wrought, and every robe was white;
On each breast bound, imperial,
The Pearl of Price with great delight.

With great delight together going
On glassy golden streets they tread;
To a hundred thousand swiftly growing,
And all alike were they garmented:
The gladdest face who could be knowing?
The Lamb did proudly pass ahead,
His seven horns of clear red gold glowing,
His robes like pearls high valuèd.
On toward the throne their way they thread,
None crowded in that band so bright,
But mild as maidens when mass is said,
So fared they forth with great delight.

The great delight His coming gave,
It were too much for me to tell.
When He approached the Elders grave,
Prone there before His feet they fell;
Legions of summoned angels brave
Swayed censers of the sweetest smell;
With music like a mighty wave,
All sang in praise of that gay Jewel.
The hymn might strike through earth to hell
That with joy those hosts of heaven recite;

To praise the Lamb I liked full well,
Amid the group in great delight. . . .

Delight that flooded eye and ear
My mortal mind beatified;
When I saw her, I must reach my dear,
Though she beyond the brook abide.
Nothing, I thought, could keep me here,
No crippling blow hold my strength tied;
I would plunge, whatever interfere,
And swim the stream, though there I died.
But ere the water I had tried,
Even as I would my vow fulfill,
From my purpose I was turned aside;
It was not to my Prince's will.

My wilful purpose pleased not Him,
That I with headlong zeal essayed;
Though I was rash of thought and limb,
Yet suddenly my deed was stayed.
As I sprang forward to the brim,
The action in my dreaming made
Me waken in my arbour trim.
My head upon the mound was laid
Where my pearl to the grass once strayed.
I stretched my body, frightened, chill,
And, sighing, to myself I said:
"Now all be to the Prince's will."

Against my will was I exiled
From that bright region, fair and fain,
From that life, glad and undefiled,
And longing dulled my sense again;
I swooned in sorrow for the child,
Needs must my heart cry and complain:
"O Pearl, dear was thy counsel mild,
In this true vision of my brain!
If very truth divide us twain;
If thou goest crowned, secure from ill,

Well for me in my prison-pain
That thou art to the Prince's will."

To the Prince's will had my heart bent,
And sought but what to me was given,
Held fast to that, with true intent,
As my Pearl prayed me out of heaven;
Did I to God my thoughts present,
More in His mysteries had I thriven.
But a man will seek more than is sent,
Till from his hand his hope be riven.
Thus from my joy was I forth driven,
From the life upon that holy hill.
Oh, fools, that with the Lord have striven,
Or proffered gifts against his will!

The Prince's will to serve aright
The Christian may full well divine;
For I have found Him, day and night,
A God, a Lord, a Friend in fine.
Upon this mound my soul hath sight,
Where I for piteous sorrow pine;
My Pearl to God I pledge and plight,
With Christ's dear blessing and with mine, –
His, who, in form of bread and wine,
The priest doth daily show us still.
His servants may we be, or shine,
Pure pearls, according to his will.

RECOMMENDED RESOURCES

Simon Armitage, *Pearl: A New Verse Translation*. This is a solid translation that is also fresh and accessible to the modern reader. (The fact that it has the Middle English original on facing pages is a nice plus.) It also includes an introduction.

J.R.R. Tolkien, *Sir Gawain and the Green Knight, Pearl, and Sir Orfeo*. This is a tour de force of translation, as Tolkien has retained the incredibly complex rhyme scheme of the poem. It's a beautiful as well as an extremely accurate translation, but its somewhat elevated syntax and word choice makes it slightly less accessible to readers who are unfamiliar with poetry. One benefit of this edition is that it's available in an inexpensive paperback, with two other excellent poems also translated by Tolkien.

QUESTIONS FOR DISCUSSION

1. What is the significance of the narrator's grief in this poem? How does it shape our understanding of the rest of the poem?

2. The glimpse of heaven that we see in *Pearl* is framed in a dream vision and makes use of allegory and symbolic imagery. What does this imagery tell us about what heaven is like?

3. We learn that Pearl was a very small child, under two years old, when she died. How does this relate to her presentation of the parable of the vineyard?

4. What does it mean for Mary to be called the "Queen of courtesy"?

5. Why can't the narrator cross the stream? What does he learn from this on his waking?

6. It is not uncommon for people to admit that their image of heaven is dull and unattractive, and to be troubled by this (since they don't find heaven attractive) and even doubt their faith. How can a poem like *Pearl* help with this?

7. Pearl touches on issues both of justice and of mercy. Discuss.

USING THE ARTS

1. Find artwork that depicts various visions or interpretations of heaven. Share and discuss: What images or themes do they have in common? How are they different? What do they show us about heaven?

2. Have students find and share music, art, or imagery that provides a 'glimpse of heaven.' Share and discuss.

Chapter Five

LATE MEDIEVAL LITERATURE

Backgrounds and Context: Dante's *Divine Comedy*

We conclude our literary journey with the *Divine Comedy*, one of the great masterpieces of world literature. An epic poem both in length and in subject matter, it takes readers through hell and then purgatory before finally arriving at a vision of the Trinity in heaven. With the classical poet Virgil appearing as an important character in the poem, it provides a link back to ancient literature; chronologically, it falls at the end of the medieval period; and thematically, it addresses a perennially relevant topic: the journey of the individual person toward God. It is both a vividly imagined story and a profound exposition of Catholic theology and doctrine.

The author is Dante Alighieri, born ca. 1265 in Florence, Italy, a center for art, culture, and cutthroat politics. Dante was involved in politics all his life and ended up paying the price for it, spending much of his life in exile from his beloved city. The *Commedia*, as Dante called it, was originally written in Italian, and Dante is considered the father of the Italian language for having written an epic poem in the vernacular at a time when Latin was still the primary language for serious literature. He worked on the poem for years, finally completing it in 1320, a year before his death.

Given the seriousness of its content, the name *comedy* can be a bit confusing, so it is helpful to know that here we find the older literary sense of *comedy*: a story that has a happy ending. What we have in the *Divine Comedy* is the preeminent happy ending, because Dante, after going through hell and purgatory, ends up in the presence of God. What happier ending is possible?

The *Divine Comedy* has three parts: *Inferno*, *Purgatorio*, and *Paradiso*, or hell, purgatory, and heaven. It is, however, one poem, not three. It's a sad mistake to read only the first part of the poem, as is very common in literature classes; to do so is to miss the point of the work as a whole. Each part is divided into thirty-three cantos, which make for easy units of reading. *Inferno* has an introductory canto, which brings the total for the Divine Comedy up to a round one hundred cantos, a numerical completeness that itself symbolizes the completeness of the spiritual journey we experience in the poem.

The poem itself is structured as a dream vision, as in "The Dream of the Rood." Here, we find that Dante himself is the main character, allowing for the poem to be narrated in the first person. We meet him as he finds himself in a dark wood, halfway through his life; he desires to get onto the right path, but he is attacked by wild animals and gets lost. In allegorical terms, his sins are keeping him from making his way toward God. However, at the heavenly intercession of Beatrice (a woman whom Dante had seen and instantly loved as a boy, and who stands as an image of God's grace), Dante is given a guide to lead him on his way. This guide is Virgil, the author of the *Aeneid*; together, they journey all the way down through hell, and then upward through purgatory. At that point Virgil, who in the allegory represents reason unaided by grace, can go no farther; Beatrice now becomes Dante's guide, and they go all the way up through heaven. Along the way, we have countless sights, experiences, and discussions that illuminate what it means to recognize sin for what it really is, repent of it, and love God.

Two words that describe the *Divine Comedy* well are 'prophetic' and 'allegorical.' Here, *prophetic* is used in the Old Testament sense, the way that Isaiah and Jeremiah were prophetic: Dante is calling his contemporaries to repent. Italy is deeply fractured and corrupt at this time, in both the political establishment and the Church. Throughout all three books of the *Divine Comedy*, we see a deep concern with politics, government, law, and the right behavior of rulers, such that some editions supply numerous footnotes to explain all the references. Dante's specific political concerns are not relevant to us now except as a matter of historical interest, but his larger point is that if Jesus is Lord, he is Lord now, not just when we die, and he is Lord of all areas of our lives, both public and private. If we truly believe what we confess as Christians, then disorder in the world, including injustice and corruption in government, is something that we have to take seriously. Even though the specific details of politics can wash over us as we read, we should attend to Dante's prophetic challenge: Do we take Christ's lordship seriously?

As an allegory, the *Divine Comedy* is, among other things, a representation of the spiritual journey of each individual person in life. On the literal level, Dante-the-character is journeying through a particular landscape; at the same time, on the allegorical level, all these places map the journey of the human soul toward God (or away from him) during life. Because the poem is written from a first-person perspective, Dante-the-character functions as an everyman figure. Any one of us can put ourselves into that space, that "I" in the poem, and see what this journey through hell, purgatory, and heaven shows us about our own spiritual growth and choices.

Dante did indeed believe in the reality of hell as the final destination for the damned, purgatory for those died in friendship with God but still needed to complete penance and purification, and then heaven for all (either directly or via purgatory) the saved. However, the poem is not an attempt to describe these places literally. The dream-vision structure of the poem gives him freedom to create an imaginative picture that communicates his larger ideas – for instance, about our relationship to God, reason and faith, justice and love, and the need for repentance and conversion. The specific details of hell, purgatory, and heaven should be recognized as Dante's own imaginative invention – not a statement about what the afterlife is 'really like.'

Therefore, when Dante names specific, real people as inhabitants of hell, he is not saying that he knows for a fact that they are there (only God knows; indeed, in the *Purgatorio*, Dante includes many reminders that conversions at the point of death are possible). Rather, he is making a pointed political commentary and also reminding the reader that what we do in our earthly lives has eternal consequences.

Dante continually underscores the fact that the *Comedy* is a *vision* of hell, purgatory, and heaven, not a literal experience of it, through the use of a living character: although Virgil is a shade, and Beatrice a blessed soul, Dante-the-character is a flesh-and-blood man who is recognized as being out of place in his journey.

The whole arc of the *Divine Comedy* moves to help the reader turn toward God. Fittingly, the whole structure of the *Divine Comedy* also corresponds to the arc of salvation history. *Inferno* is the equivalent of Egypt, with the Israelites in bondage. *Purgatorio* corresponds to the wilderness: God leads them out of Egypt, but they're not ready yet to enter the Promised Land. *Paradiso* represents the Promised Land, where they're able to go when they're finally ready.

First, in *Inferno*, we see the true ugliness of sin, stripped of any partial goods associated with it. Thus, as part of the spiritual journey, Dante is helping us to see sin rightly and reject it, to acknowledge our own weakness, and recognize our own inability to save ourselves. In *Purgatorio*, we explore how we are sanctified. Simply rejecting sin doesn't make us instantly holy. Rather, in Dante's poem, we see how we grow in holiness by cooperating with God's grace acting in us.

Finally, we explore what it means to *be* holy, discovering that goodness and holiness are not dull and static, but dynamic and vibrant. Here we have the whole spiritual journey, from repentance, confession, and conversion through the process of sanctification, as we become more and more Christ-like.

Inferno

As we go on this allegorical journey, we will see that the horrors of hell, the sufferings of purgatory, and the joys of heaven are not arbitrary punishments and rewards by a fickle and inscrutable God. This makes the *Divine Comedy* particularly important for evangelization and discipleship, because many people are kept from a serious consideration of Christianity by a fundamental misconception about what Christians believe: the idea that the God we worship condemns people to eternal punishment merely for not knowing about him, or that our entrance into heaven is earned by doing the right things.

Dante, in taking us through this journey, challenges us as Christian readers to examine the way we present God's judgment and love. What we see in this spiritual journey is that hell and heaven, far from being arbitrary, are actually the natural end result of our own choices. We choose what we really want. Do we want God? Then our choices will turn us toward him, and we can accept his offer of grace. To be clear: Dante is not suggesting that we can save ourselves, but he is consistent with Catholic theology in saying that we can choose to respond to, or reject, God's offered grace, which we cannot earn or merit on our own.

In *Inferno*, Dante arranges the levels of hell in terms of seriousness of sin, drawing to a certain extent on Christian tradition about the seven deadly sins, but he is not making a claim about the exact punishments for every sin. (It is also worth noting that although the idea of Limbo was put forth by some early Christian theologians, such as St. Augustine of Hippo, and became part of popular imagination, it is not part of Catholic doctrine. Dante may or may not have believed in Limbo himself, but at any rate, it is an imaginatively useful image for a certain spiritual condition.) Rather, Dante is drawing our attention to the real consequences of sin. In our individualistic modern culture, we tend to be very self-centered, but in truth, it's *not* just about me and my relationship with Jesus, and, in secular terms, the actions of two consenting adults *does* have an effect beyond those two consenting adults. Our sin hurts ourselves, it hurts other people, and it hurts our culture and society – that's what Dante is calling us to see.

The emphasis on the final result of human choices in the *Divine Comedy* is particularly helpful in our post-Christian culture. We live in a world full of common grace, in which God gives many good things to everyone. Both those who do good and those who do evil can enjoy the sunshine. It is easy to forget, or never realize, that every good thing comes from God, whether it's a cup of coffee or the happiness that comes from being with family – any pleasure or joy of any kind. If we turn to God, we are turning to the source of all good. If we reject him, then by definition we are turning from all good. *All of it.* We are left alone with ourselves: the condition that is, by definition, hell. God doesn't 'send' anyone to hell against their will. The state of rejecting all that is good is in itself as bad as you can get.

As we go through hell, it is important to note that Dante's depiction highlights the sin and not the sinner. Hell is populated by characters who, because of their rejection of God, are now reduced to the essence of their sin, and it is an ugly and disturbing sight. In life, sin is so often disguised, excused, or delayed in its effects that we can become blind to it, but Dante helps us to see sin for the ugly thing that it is.

In the first canto of *Inferno*, we meet Dante-the-character in a dark wood. He has tried to climb the straight path up the mountain (allegorically, toward God) and has been prevented from doing so by three wild animals: a leopard representing lust (self-indulgent sins, not necessarily only sexual), a lion representing pride (sins that stem from a desire to be in control), and a wolf representing greed (sins of envy and covetousness). All these are sins that ordinary people struggle with, even those who are on the right path to God. The difference is that Dante has been lost in this dark wood: his sins have been left to run wild, so to speak, and have gained in strength. The small temptations that were not resisted, and the small sins that were not repented of, are no longer, as it were, leopard kittens and wolf puppies. They have grown up to become so strong that they prevent him from going on the straight path to God.

At this point, Dante is stuck, and good intentions are not enough to get him back on the right track. Right from the start, then, we see that sin is not just some item on an arbitrary 'no' list; sins are those things that stand between us and God.

At this point in the story, Dante encounters a ghost: the shade or spirit of the Roman poet Virgil, who introduces himself and proposes to lead Dante on a different path: through hell, through purgatory, to heaven. It's a grueling journey for Dante and for the reader alike, but a valuable one.

SELECTION

Excerpt from *Inferno*

From *The Divine Comedy of Dante Alighieri*,
translated by Courtney Langdon

CANTO I

The Wood and the Mountain

When half way through the journey of our life
I found that I was in a gloomy wood,
because the path which led aright was lost.
And ah, how hard it is to say just what
this wild and rough and stubborn woodland was,
the very thought of which renews my fear!
So bitter 't is, that death is little worse;
but of the good to treat which there I found,
I'll speak of what I else discovered there.

I cannot well say how I entered it,
so full of slumber was I at the moment
when I forsook the pathway of the truth;
but after I had reached a mountain's foot,
where that vale ended which had pierced my heart
with fear, I looked on high, and saw its shoulders
mantled already with that planet's rays
which leadeth one aright o'er every path.

Then quieted a little was the fear,
which in the lake-depths of my heart had lasted
throughout the night I passed so piteously.

And even as he who, from the deep emerged
with sorely troubled breath upon the shore,
turns round, and gazes at the dangerous water;
even so my mind, which still was fleeing on,

turned back to look again upon the pass
which ne'er permitted any one to live.
When I had somewhat eased my weary body,
o'er the lone slope I so resumed my way,
that e'er the lower was my steady foot.
Then lo, not far from where the ascent began,
a Leopard which, exceeding light and swift,
was covered over with a spotted hide,
and from my presence did not move away;
nay, rather, she so hindered my advance,
that more than once I turned me to go back.
Some time had now from early morn elapsed,
and with those very stars the sun was rising
that in his escort were, when Love Divine
in the beginning moved those beauteous things;
I therefore had as cause for hoping well
of that wild beast with gaily mottled skin,
the hour of daytime and the year's sweet season;
but not so, that I should not fear the sight,
which next appeared before me, of a Lion,
– against me this one seemed to be advancing
with head erect and with such raging hunger,
that even the air seemed terrified thereby –
and of a she-Wolf, which with every lust
seemed in her leanness laden, and had caused
many ere now to lead unhappy lives.
The latter so oppressed me with the fear
that issued from her aspect, that I lost
the hope I had of winning to the top.
And such as he is, who is glad to gain,
and who, when times arrive that make him lose,
weeps and is saddened in his every thought;
such did that peaceless animal make me,
which, 'gainst me coming, pushed me, step by step,
back to the place where silent is the sun.
While toward the lowland I was falling fast,
the sight of one was offered to mine eyes,
who seemed, through long continued silence, weak.
When him in that vast wilderness I saw,

"Have pity on me," I cried out to him,
"whate'er thou be, or shade, or very man!"
"Not man," he answered, "I was once a man;
and both my parents were of Lombardy,
and Mantuans with respect to fatherland.
'Neath Julius was I born, though somewhat late,
and under good Augustus' rule I lived
in Rome, in days of false and lying gods.
I was a poet, and of that just man,
Anchises' son, I sang, who came from Troy
after proud Ilion had been consumed.
But thou, to such sore trouble why return?
Why climbst thou not the Mountain of Delight,
which is of every joy the source and cause?"
"Art thou that Virgil, then, that fountain-head
which poureth forth so broad a stream of speech?"
I answered him with shame upon my brow.
"O light and glory of the other poets,
let the long study, and the ardent love
which made me con thy book, avail me now.
Thou art my teacher and authority;
thou only art the one from whom I took
the lovely manner which hath done me honor.
Behold the beast on whose account I turned;
from her protect me, O thou famous Sage,
for she makes both my veins and pulses tremble!"
"A different course from this must thou pursue,"
he answered, when he saw me shedding tears,
"if from this wilderness thou wouldst escape;
for this wild beast, on whose account thou criest,
alloweth none to pass along her way,
but hinders him so greatly, that she kills;
and is by nature so malign and guilty,
that never doth she sate her greedy lust,
but after food is hungrier than before.
Many are the animals with which she mates,
and still more will there be, until the Hound
shall come, and bring her to a painful death.
He shall not feed on either land or wealth,

but wisdom, love and power shall be his food,
and 'tween two Feltros shall his birth take place.
Of that low Italy he'll be the savior,
for which the maid Camilla died of wounds,
with Turnus, Nisus and Eurỳalus.
And he shall drive her out of every town,
till he have put her back again in Hell,
from which the earliest envy sent her forth.

I therefore think and judge it best for thee
to follow me; and I shall be thy guide,
and lead thee hence through an eternal place,
where thou shalt hear the shrieks of hopelessness
of those tormented spirits of old times,
each one of whom bewails the second death;
then those shalt thou behold who, though in fire,
contented are, because they hope to come,
whene'er it be, unto the blessèd folk;
to whom, thereafter, if thou wouldst ascend,
there'll be for that a worthier soul than I.
With her at my departure I shall leave thee,
because the Emperor who rules up there,
since I was not obedient to His law,
wills none shall come into His town through me.
He rules as emperor everywhere, and there
as king; there is His town and lofty throne.
O happy he whom He thereto elects!"

And I to him: "O Poet, I beseech thee,
even by the God it was not thine to know,
so may I from this ill and worse escape,
conduct me thither where thou saidst just now,
that I may see Saint Peter's Gate, and those
whom thou describest as so whelmed with woe."
He then moved on, and I behind him kept.

CANTO VII

The Fourth Circle. Intemperance in Wealth. Misers and Prodigals. The Fifth Circle

"*Papè Satàn, papè Satàn, alèppë!*"
thus Plutus with his clucking voice began;
that noble Sage, then, who knew everything,
said, to encourage me: "Let not thy fear
distress thee, for, whatever power he have,
he'll not prevent our going down this rock."
Then to those swollen lips he turned around,
and said: "Be silent, thou accursèd wolf;
with thine own rage consume thyself within!
Not causeless is our going to the bottom;
there is it willed on high, where Michael wrought
vengeance upon the arrogant rebellion."
As sails, when swollen by the wind, fall down
entangled, when the mast breaks; even so,
down to the ground the cruel monster fell.
Into the fourth ditch we descended thus,
advancing further o'er the woeful edge,
which bags all evil in the universe.
Justice of God, alas! who heapeth up
the many unheard of toils and pains I saw,
and wherefore doth our sin torment us so?
As yonder o'er Charybdis doth the sea,
which breaks against the one it runs to meet,
so must the people dance a ring-dance here.
I here saw folk, more numerous than elsewhere,
on one side and the other, with great howls
rolling big weights around by strength of chest;
they struck against each other; then, right there
each turned, and rolling back his weight, cried out:
"Why keepest thou?" and "Wherefore throw away?"
They circled thus around the gloomy ring
on either hand unto the point opposed,
still shouting each to each their vile refrain;

then each turned back, when through his own half-ring
he had attained the other butting place. . . .
We crossed the circle to the other bank
over a bubbling stream, that poureth down
along a ditch which from it takes its shape.
Than purple-black much darker was its water;
and we, accompanying its dusky waves,
went down and entered on an uncouth path.
A swamp it forms which hath the name of Styx,
this dismal little brook, when it hath reached
the bottom of the grey, malignant slopes.
And I, who was intensely gazing there,
saw muddy people in that slimy marsh,
all naked, and with anger in their looks.
They struck each other, not with hands alone,
but with their heads and chests, and with their feet,
and rent each other piecemeal with their teeth.
Said the good Teacher: "Son, thou seest now
the souls of those whom anger overcame;
nay, more, I'd have thee certainly believe
that 'neath the water there are folk who sigh,
and make this water bubble at its surface,
as, wheresoe'er it turn, thine eye reveals.
Stuck in the slime, they say: "Sullen we were
in the sweet air that's gladdened by the sun,
bearing within us fumes of surliness;
we now are sullen in the swamp's black mire."
This hymn they gurgle down inside their throats,
because they cannot utter it with perfect speech.
And so we circled round the filthy fen
a great arc 'tween the dry bank and the marsh,
our eyes intent on those that swallow mud;
and to a tower's foot we came at last.

RECOMMENDED RESOURCES

Anthony Esolen, *Inferno, Purgatory,* and *Paradise,* Modern Library edition. This good, readable translation is especially valuable for its extensive notes by Esolen, a Catholic scholar, and illustrations by Gustave Doré.

Robin Kirkpatrick, *The Divine Comedy.* Kirkpatrick's translation is also excellent, and the Flame Tree Collections edition is particularly good, with Gustave Doré's illustrations.

Robert Hollander and Jean Hollander, *Inferno, Purgatorio,* and *Paradiso.* Another good and readable translation.

Dorothy L. Sayers, *Hell, Purgatory,* and *Heaven.* It is well worth getting a copy of Sayers' translations just for her introductions and notes, which are exceptionally good. However, I do not recommend it for the translation. Sayers attempted to reproduce the same rhyme scheme as in the Italian, but since English has much less rhyming flexibility than Italian, the result is rather stilted.

Fr. Paul Pearson of the Oratory, *Spiritual Direction from Dante: Avoiding the Inferno.* Fr. Pearson's series is an insightful, detailed look at the spiritual lessons to be gained from Dante's poem.

Peter J. Leithart, *Ascent to Love: A Guide to Dante's Divine Comedy.*

Peter Hainsworth and David Robey, *Dante: A Very Short Introduction.*

QUESTIONS FOR DISCUSSION

1. What does it mean to be lost in the 'gloomy wood'?

2. How does the journey through hell correspond with the sacrament of Reconciliation (Confession)?

3. Dante chooses punishments that correspond to the spiritual significance of the sin. Choose one or two of these to discuss.

4. In *Inferno*, the structure of hell is such that the severity of the sin and its punishment increase as one goes downward. In Dante's placement, the sins of the spirit, such as pride, are much more serious than the sins of the body, such as adultery or gluttony. Discuss.

5. Dante places heretics in hell. What is the difference between deliberate heresy and being in error?

6. Dante places in hell those who commit suicide. This is a very sensitive topic, and this portion of the *Inferno* can be deeply troubling. It is, however, a pastorally important issue, especially with the rise of 'assisted suicide' as socially acceptable. What does Dante's depiction show us about the wrongness of suicide or self-harm in general? What additional psychological, emotional, and pastoral considerations should enter into our handling of this topic, especially with those who are tempted toward suicide?

7. In *Inferno*, the deepest layer of hell is icy cold, with sinners frozen in ice. What does this show us about the effect of sin on the soul?

8. The name of Christ is never spoken in hell. Discuss.

USING THE ARTS

1. Look at illustrations of specific scenes in *Inferno* – for instance, in the engravings by Gustave Doré or Botticelli. How does the image give new insight into the sin being represented?

2. Dante-the-character is unable to head directly upward (allegorically, toward God) because his way is blocked by three fierce animals: a leopard, a lion, and a wolf. What animals might represent the sins that prevent you from growing closer to God? Illustrate them.

Purgatorio

Although Dante's *Inferno* is the most familiar part of the *Divine Comedy* for most readers, *Purgatorio* is perhaps even more important as a source of discussion for evangelization and discipleship today.

Each of the levels of purgatory deals with one of the seven deadly sins: pride, envy, anger, sloth (or *acedia* – spiritual apathy – which is the better term for it), greed, gluttony, and lust. The physical geography of purgatory is the exact inverse of hell. Whereas hell was a funnel leading downward, purgatory is a cone-shaped mountain with its levels corresponding to the same sins as in hell, but in reverse order. In purgatory, the more serious sins have greater weight, holding the penitent down from climbing up the mountain. The spiritual sins dealt with at the bottom of Mount Purgatory (pride, envy, anger, and acedia) are thus seen to have left stronger marks on the soul than the sins of incontinence (greed, gluttony, and lust: right desires wrongly oriented, or desires for good things expressed in excess).

Dante's representation of purgatory makes it clear that it is a place of penance and preparation for saved souls, not a 'second chance' at salvation. We can (and should) hope that a sinner repents at the moment of death, but if someone dies in a state of separation from God, then that person goes to hell, and there are no second chances. Those who have turned to Christ, even at the last minute, are all destined for heaven – but everyone except the very holiest of men and women needs to spend some time in purgatory after death for sanctification to be completed; all their sins are forgiven, but some penance may still remain to be done, and the soul may still need to be healed of the *effects* of sin.

Though purgatory is a place of penance, Dante shows it as a place full of songs of praise and joy. Here we can see him contributing to an imaginative recovery of a right view of purgatory. While Catholic teaching does not specify what the experience of purgatory is like for the souls in it, by the end of the medieval period purgatory had taken on such negative associations in the popular imagination that the souls in purgatory were considered to experience torments similar to those of the damned. Although this darker view rightly stressed the seriousness of sin, it could also encourage fear rather than hope in one's anticipation of life after death. Dante's *Purgatorio* is, therefore, a helpful imaginative corrective; his representation of purgatory shows the suffering here as cleansing and healing.

Dante's dream-vision structure turns out to be particularly important here. The souls that Dante meets on his journey through purgatory are all saved souls, but he, unlike them, is a living man, experiencing this journey in a vision. As readers, we are in exactly the same situation as Dante-the-character: we are living human beings who are still working out our salvation with fear and trembling, as St. Paul puts it, in this earthly life. What stains of sin would need to be removed from our souls, if we died now? How much sanctification do we still require? His imagined purgatory helps us move toward repentance, conversion, and growth in holiness, just as his imagined hell helps the reader be moved to reject sin.

At the end of *Purgatorio*, Dante and Virgil arrive at the summit of purgatory, the Garden of Earthly Delight, where Dante meets Beatrice. Allegorically, Dante is an everyman figure, representing the human soul, the pagan poet Virgil represents human reason, and Beatrice represents God's grace. The cooperation of Virgil and Beatrice shows that grace and reason both have a part to play in the journey of faith. Virgil, who is representative of reason and philosophy, can take us a long way, perhaps even to the gates of heaven – but not all the way. Divine grace is needed, not to replace human reason but to build on it.

Here, Dante suggests the right relationship between the intellect and grace. Intellect (itself a gift of God) helps him arrive at the place where he can be touched directly by grace. When Dante was in the dark wood, Beatrice expressed her desire to reach him and guide him into heaven, but he was too lost to be able to hear her directly. The intellect, itself moved by grace (represented by Virgil who has been summoned to the task by Beatrice) guides Dante to a place where he can hear Beatrice and where he can experience God's grace directly.

When Virgil hands Dante over to the care entirely of Beatrice, we see something important about the Christian life: we can't love God just by knowing *about* him. Philosophy and theology can teach us about God, but that's not the same thing as knowing him personally, loving him, and obeying him. Thus, here we have Beatrice coming in as the guide of grace to enable Dante to take that further step into an active relationship with God. Dante does not dismiss the role of reason, but he shows that faith, acting in obedience and love, is a step beyond reason, though certainly not in contradiction to it.

SELECTION

Excerpt from *Purgatorio*

From *The Divine Comedy of Dante Alighieri*,
translated by Courtney Langdon

CANTO I

Antepurgatory. The Vale of Flowers. Dante's First Dream. The Gate of Purgatory

Already was old Titan's concubine
whitening upon the Orient's balcony,
outside the arms of her sweet paramour;
already was her forehead shining bright
with gems, arranged according to the shape
of that cold beast, which smites one with its tail;
and Night had of the steps wherewith she climbs,
already taken two where we were then,
and now the third was lowering its wings;
when I, who had somewhat of Adam in me,
o'ercome with sleep, reclined upon the grass,
on which all five of us were sitting then.
Near morning, at the hour in which the swallow
begins to sing her melancholy lays,
perchance in memory of her earliest woes,
and when, much more a pilgrim from the flesh,
and less imprisoned by its thoughts, our mind
well nigh prophetic in its vision is;
an Eagle in a dream I seemed to see
suspended in the sky, with plumes of gold
and wings outspread, intent on swooping down;
and it appeared to me that I was where
his friends were left behind by Ganymede,
when to the highest council he was raised.

I thought within myself: "Perhaps this bird
is wont to strike but here, and from elsewhere,
perhaps, disdains to lift one with its claws."
Then, having wheeled a while, it seemed to me
that terrible as lightning it came down,
and bore me up as far as to the fire.
There it and I both seemed to burn together;
and so intense was that imagined burning,
my sleep was broken of necessity.
Achilles roused himself no differently –
turning around him his awakened eyes,
nor knowing in what region he might be,
when, sleeping in her arms, his mother took him
away from Chiron to the isle of Scyros,
from which the Greeks removed him afterwards –
than I aroused myself, when from my face
sleep fled away; and death-like pale I turned,
like one who freezes when o'ercome by fright.
Only my Comforter was at my side,
and now the sun was higher than two hours,
and toward the open sea my face was turned.
"Be not afraid!" my Lord then said to me.
"Be reassured, for we are faring well;
restrain not, but expand thine every power!
At Purgatory art thou now arrived;
behold the cliff there, which encloses it;
behold the entrance where it broken seems.
Just now, when, in the dawn preceding day,
thy soul was sleeping in thee on the flowers,
wherewith the place down yonder is adorned,
a Lady came and said: 'I am Lucìa;
allow me to take up this sleeping man;
I shall assist him thus upon his way.'
Sordello and the other noble forms
remained; she took thee, and when daylight dawned,
hither came up, and in her foot-prints I.
She laid thee here; and first her lovely eyes
revealed to me that opened entrance; then
both she and sleep together passed away."

Like one who, when in doubt, is reassured,
and into comfort turns his fear, when once
the truth has been disclosed to him, I changed;
and when my Leader wholly freed from care
beheld me, upward o'er the cliff he moved,
and I behind him followed toward the height.
Reader, thou surely see'st how I exalt
my subject; therefore be thou not surprised
if I support it now with greater art.
Nearer we drew, and were in such a place,
that where at first there seemed to be a break,
just like a fissure that divides a wall,
I saw a Gate, and under, to approach it,
three steps of different color each, and then
a Keeper, who as yet said not a word.
And as I opened more and more mine eyes,
I saw him sitting on the upper step,
such in his face that I endured him not;
and in his hand he had a naked sword,
which so reflected upon us its rays,
that toward him oft I turned my eyes in vain.
"Say what it is you wish, from where you are,"
he then began, "and where your escort is.
Beware lest coming up should do you harm."
"A heavenly Lady, of these things aware,"
my Teacher answered him, "said unto us
just now: 'Go thither, yonder is the Gate.'"
"And unto good may she advance your steps!"
the courteous Keeper of the Gate resumed,
"Come forward, therefore, unto these our stairs."
Made of white marble was the first great step
to which we came, so polished and so smooth,
I mirrored me therein as I appear.
The second step, darker than purple-black,
was of a rough and calcined kind of stone,
cracked lengthwise and across. The third, which rests
in massive shape above it, seemed to me
to be of porphyry as flaming red,
as blood appears when spurting from a vein.

Upon this last God's Angel held both feet,
sitting upon the threshold, which to me
appeared to be a rock of adamant.
Up over those three steps my Leader then
drew me along with my good will, and said:
"Humbly request him to undo the lock."
Devoutly at his holy feet I cast me;
I begged that of his mercy he would open,
but first I smote upon my breast three times.
Then with his sword's sharp point he traced seven P's
upon my brow, and told me: "See thou to it,
that, when inside, thou wash away these wounds!"
Ashes, or earth when excavated dry,
would with his garment of one color be;
and from beneath it he drew forth two Keys.
One was of gold, the other silver was;
first with the white, and after with the yellow,
he so did to the Gate that I was pleased.
"Whenever one of these Keys faileth so,
that in the lock it doth not rightly turn,"
said he to us, "this passage opens not.
More precious is the first; and yet the other,
ere it unlock, much skill and judgment needs,
for it is that one which unties the knot.
Peter, from whom I hold them, bade me err
rather in opening, than in keeping closed,
provided folk fell prostrate at my feet."
He pushed the holy Portal's door thereat,
and said to us: "Go in; but I inform you
that he who looks behind returns outside."
And when that sacred Gateway's folding doors,
which were of strong resounding metal made,
were on their iron hinges turned around,
Tarpeia roared not so, nor proved so shrill,
when good Metellus was removed from her,
because of which she afterwards kept lean.
I turned to heed its first resounding tones,
and "*Thee we praise, O Lord*" I seemed to hear
in voices mixed with those delightful sounds.

What I was hearing made upon me then
just the impression one is wont to get,
when people with an organ sing; for now
the words are heard, and now again are not.

CANTO X – XI

Purgatory. The First Ring. Pride. The Expiation of Pride.

. . . "On this side, lo,
much people come, but slow the steps they take;"
the Poet murmured, "toward the grades above
these souls will send us forward on our way."
Mine eyes, intent on gazing, to behold
new things, for which with eagerness they long,
in turning toward him were not slow to move.
Yet I'd not have thee, Reader, shrink dismayed
from thy good purposes, through hearing how
God wills that what is due be paid. Heed not
the nature of the torment! Think of what
comes after! Think that, at the very worst,
beyond the Judgment-day it cannot go.
Then I began: "That, Teacher, which toward us
I see advancing does not look like people,
nor know I what, my sight is so deceived."
And he to me: "Their torment's heavy nature
so bows them toward the ground, that my eyes, too,
struggled therewith at first. But steadily
gaze there, and disentangle with thine eyes
what underneath those stones is coming on;
thou now canst see how each one smites himself."
O ye proud Christians, sad and weary creatures,
who, sick in mental vision, put your trust
in backward moving steps; perceive ye not
that worms we are, created but to form
the angelic butterfly, which flies unscreened

to judgment? Why, then, is it that your mind
soars up in pride, since ye are, as it were,
defective insects, even as is a worm,
in which formation is not yet complete?
As, to hold up a ceiling or a roof,
in lieu of corbel, one perceives at times
a human figure joining knees to breast,
which out of unreality gives birth
to real distress in him who sees it; such
seemed these to me, when I had given good heed.
They were, in truth, both more and less bowed down,
as each had more or less upon his back;
but he that in his acts most patient was,
seemed to say, weeping: "I can bear no more!"

CANTO XI

Purgatory. The First Ring. Pride. The Lord's Prayer.

"Our Father, Thou that in the Heavens dost dwell,
not circumscribed, but for the greater love
Thou hast for what Thou madest first on high;
let both Thy Name and Worth be given praise
by every creature, ev'n as it is meet
that to Thy loving Spirit thanks be given!
And may Thy Kingdom's Peace come down to us,
since we can not attain it of ourselves,
for all our striving, save it also come!
As gladly of their wills Thine Angels make
a sacrifice to Thee, singing 'All Hail!',
so likewise gladly may men do with theirs!
Give us this day our daily spirit-food,
without which, through this bitter wilderness,
he backward goes, who onward toileth most!
And as we pardon every one the wrong
we've suffered, of Thy Mercy do Thou us

forgive, regarding not what we deserve!
Our virtue which is easily o'ercome,
test Thou not through our ancient Enemy,
but set us free from him, who tempts it so!
This last request, dear Lord, is not, indeed,
made for ourselves, who need not make it here,
but is for their sake who behind us stayed."

Thus praying good speed for themselves and us,
those shades beneath a burden went their way,
not unlike that whereof one dreams at times,
unequally tormented, all of them,
and weary, o'er the first ring, round and round,
purging away the world's defiling mists.

RECOMMENDED RESOURCES

For suggested translations, see *Inferno.*

Fr. Paul Pearson of the Oratory, *Spiritual Direction from Dante: Ascending Mount Purgatory.* As with the previous volume on *Inferno*, Fr. Pearson's guide unpacks the spiritual significance of the poem.

QUESTIONS FOR DISCUSSION

1. What was your image of purgatory before reading *Purgatorio*? Has the poem changed this image in any way?

2. What do the respective roles of Virgil and Beatrice suggest about the process of evangelization? How can we help natural reason to be receptive to grace?

3. What does the entrance to purgatory show about the need for humility and repentance?

4. The seven "P"s inscribed on Dante's forehead stand for *Peccatum* (Latin for 'sin') and thus represent the marks caused by these sins, which need to be scrubbed away. How is it that sin (which has been repented of) can leave a mark on one's own soul?

5. Compare the punishments in canto VII of *Inferno* with the penances of canto X of *Purgatorio*. What is the spiritual difference between the two scenes?

6. Why did Dante need to go through hell before he could begin the ascent of Mount Purgatory?

7. How is Dante's entrance into purgatory different from the start of his journey in the dark wood?

USING THE ARTS

1. Throughout the *Purgatorio*, Dante comes across carved scenes that illustrate the virtues. For instance, in the first part of canto X, he sees a carving that represents Mary at the Annunciation. Have participants draw one or more of these scenes. For a more advanced group, set up a *tableau vivant* with participants acting out the scene in question.

2. Write expansions of prayers, as we see with the souls of the proud singing the Our Father.

3. At various points in both *Inferno* and *Purgatorio*, Dante has conversations with souls there. Have participants create and act out dialogues dealing with the same sin: with an unrepentant soul in hell, and with a repentant soul in purgatory.

Paradiso

In *Paradiso*, Dante faces his greatest imaginative challenge: showing us heaven. Of course, he falls short; the imagination of a fallen man is not capable of expressing the fullness of heaven.

As we consider the imagined geography of heaven, we should note that Dante presents heaven as it is *before* the general resurrection; thus, it is appropriate that the saints don't have bodies – they are waiting for them. Since we do not yet have a new heaven and a new earth, Dante's heaven works entirely within the structure of medieval cosmology. Here we have ten 'heavens' within heaven. Seven of them are associated with what in medieval cosmology were called 'planets.' The Moon, Mercury, and Venus are the first heavens that we see; as he moves through each of these with Beatrice, he encounters saved souls whose flaws or limitations with regard to the virtues of fortitude, justice, and temperance keep them from being in the higher heavens. Next are the heavens of the Sun, Mars, Jupiter, and Saturn, where we see Dante talking with various souls who represent the fullness of the virtues of prudence, courage, justice, and temperance. When we get to the eighth heaven, we enter into the realm of the fixed stars and an exploration of the theological virtues of faith, hope, and love.

This construction of heaven allows us to think about different kinds of virtue. The 'lower' heavens showcase the natural virtues, called 'natural' because things like courage, moderation, or prudence are available to all through God's common grace. They will not be developed perfectly, but they're still available to all. Faith, hope, and love, understood in terms of Christian theology, are the three supernatural or theological virtues. That is, the fullness of faith, hope, and love are only possible through our relationship with Christ.

Dante then moves to the ninth heaven, which is called the *Primum Mobile,* where he receives a vision of creation from God's perspective. In the tenth heaven, the Empyrean, he has another vision, of the celestial dance of all the saved souls, appearing as if a rose with overlapping petals. The image may seem strange, but it calls our attention to the order and beauty and movement in heaven.

Here we can pause for a moment to consider one of the problems faced by evangelists: that even Christians may have an image of heaven that is bland, static, and frankly dull. Indeed, even in *Paradiso*, our overall impression of heaven can seem a bit too ethereal, especially in contrast with the earthier imagery of the first two parts of the poem.

It's always easier to write about (and understand what we read about) things that are familiar to us. Everyone has sinned and been harmed by sin, so when we go through the *Inferno* and the *Purgatorio* with Dante, we can relate what he is showing us to our lived experience. However, neither Dante nor any of his readers have the experience of being completely free from sin and in perfect relationship with God, so it's harder for him to find adequate images, and harder for us to imaginatively engage with the images he does find.

Nevertheless, Dante's *Paradiso* offers a richly meaningful view of heaven. In contrast to the frozen floor of hell, heaven is in constant movement, a cosmic dance. We can also see in *Paradiso* that heaven is full of variety. For example, in canto XI, Dante talks with St. Thomas Aquinas, the great theologian, who is a Dominican; St. Thomas praises St. Francis, the founder of the order of Franciscans. Then in canto XII, we find St. Bonaventure, a Franciscan, praising St. Dominic, the founder of the Dominican order. It is an image of the beautiful diversity of heaven: not for its own sake but a lively diversity of personalities and ways to be holy. In these heavenly conversations, we see a celebration of both preaching and teaching (the Dominican focus) and the care of the poor (the Franciscan focus), which combine to give us a picture of the Pauline expression of 'many members, one body.'

Another way in which Dante evokes the richness of heaven is in the conversations that he has with various blessed souls in the different spheres. It turns out that the people in heaven are interested in many of the same things as people on earth: being in heaven doesn't make people less curious or intelligent. For example, as Dante rises through the spheres, he has many conversations about science: How does the natural world work? Why did God choose the Incarnation and death of Jesus as the means of our redemption and not some other way? God's gift of reason allows us to think about these things. Dante also talks about politics – the saints are interested in the way the kingdom is being lived out in the world.

Throughout the *Paradiso*, these theological, scientific, and political discussions remind us that the desire for knowledge is good, when it's directed rightly. To be sure, the desire to learn can become a form of covetousness, where we accumulate knowledge for our own pride and satisfaction. But Dante has the right orientation; he wants to know more about God, God's creation, and the ways God has acted in the world, and in so doing, he is drawing closer to God.

SELECTION

Excerpt from *Paradiso*

From *The Divine Comedy of Dante Alighieri*,
translated by Courtney Langdon

CANTO I

Introduction to the *Paradiso*. Invocation of Apollo. Ascent through the Sphere of Fire. The Order of the Universe

The Glory of Him who moveth everything,
penetrates all the Universe, and shines
more brightly in one part, and elsewhere less.
Within the Heaven which most receives His Light
I was; and saw what he who thence descends
neither knows how, nor hath the power, to tell;
for as it draweth near to its Desire,
our intellect so deeply sinks therein,
that recollection cannot follow it.
As much, however, of the holy Realm
as in my memory I could treasure up,
shall now become the subject of my song.
O Good Apollo, for my final task
make me as worthy a vessel of Thy Power,
as Thou dost ask for Thy dear laurel's gift.
One of Parnassus' peaks hath hitherto
sufficed me; but with both of them I now
must start upon the course which still remains.
Enter my breast, and breathe Thou as of old
Thou didst, when from the scabbard of his limbs
Thou drewest Marsyas forth.
O Power Divine,
if Thou but lend Thyself to me so much,
that I may show the blessèd Kingdom's shadow

which in my mind is stamped; to Thy dear tree
Thou 'lt see me come, and crown me with the leaves
my theme and Thou shall cause me to deserve.
So seldom, Father, are there any picked,
to grace a Caesar's or a Poet's triumph,
(the fault of human wills, and to their shame),
that His Peneian leaf should bring forth joy
within the Joyous Delphic Deity,
when for itself it causes one to thirst.

A great flame follows from a little spark;
perhaps with better voices after me
shall men so pray, that Cyrrha will reply.

For mortal men the lantern of the world
rises through divers passes; but from that
which with three crosses brings four rings together,
it issues on a more propitious course,
and in conjunction with a kinder star,
and more in its own image moulds and seals
the mundane wax. A pass almost like this
had made it morning there and evening here;
and all that hemisphere was white, and black
the other side; when Beatrice I saw
turned toward her left, and looking at the sun;
no eagle ever gazed at it so keenly.

And even as from the first a second ray
is wont to come, and upward start again,
as would a pilgrim longing to return;
even so to her act, by mine eyes infused
through my imagination, mine conformed;
and on the sun I gazed beyond our wont.

Much is permitted there, which is not here
allowed our faculties, thanks to the site
created as the human race's home.

Not long did I endure it, nor so briefly,
as not to see it sparkle all around,
as molten iron doth, when out of fire
it issues boiling; day then all at once
seemed joined to day, as if the One who can
had with another sun adorned the sky.

With eyes fixed wholly on the eternal wheels
stood Beatrice; and I on her fixed mine,
from there above removed. Looking at her,
I such became within, as Glaucus did
on tasting of the herb, which in the sea
made him a fellow of the other Gods.

Transhumanizing could not be expressed
by words; let this case, therefore, him suffice,
for whom Grace holds experience in reserve.

If I, O Love that rulest Heaven, was only
that part of me, which Thou didst last create,
Thou know'st, that with Thy Light didst raise me up.

When the rotation Thou, by being longed for,
dost make eternal, drew me to itself
by harmonies distributed and tuned
by Thee, it seemed that so much of the sky
was by the sun's flame set on fire, that rain
nor river ever made so broad a lake.

The newness of the sound, and brilliant light
kindled in me a wish to know their cause,
never with so great keenness felt; whence she,
who saw me ev'n as I behold myself,
opened her mouth to calm my troubled mind,
ere I did mine to question, and began:

"With false imagining dost thou so dull
thyself, that thou perceivest not what else
thou wouldst perceive, if thou hadst thrown it off.
Thou 'rt not on earth, as thou dost think thyself;
but lightning fleeing from its proper place
ne'er ran as thou, that art thereto returning."

If I was by her little smiled-out words
of my first doubt relieved, within a new one
was I the more ensnared; I therefore said:
"Already sated, I had found repose
from great amazement; but I wonder now
how I can these light elements transcend."

Heaving, thereat, a pitying sigh, she turned
her eyes upon me with the look a mother
gives her delirious child; and then began:

"All things, whate'er they be, an order have
among themselves; and form this order is,
which makes the Universe resemble God.
Therein exalted creatures see the trace
of that Eternal Worth, which is the end
for which the mentioned order is created.
Within the ordered state whereof I speak,
all natures have their place with different lots,
as nearer to their source they are, or less;
wherefore toward different ports they wend their way
through the vast sea of being, each endowed
with instinct, granted it to bear it on.
This instinct toward the moon impelleth fire;
this is the motive force in mortal hearts;
this binds together and unites the earth;
nor doth this bow impel those creatures only
which lack intelligence, but those that have
intelligence and love. The Providence
which ordereth all this, with Its own Light
e'er calms the heaven, inside of which revolves
the one that moveth with the greatest speed.
And thither now, as to a place ordained,
that bowstring's power is bearing us along,
which to a glad mark speeds whate'er it shoots.
'T is true that, as a form is frequently
discordant with the intention of an art,
because its matter in response is deaf;
so likewise from this natural course at times
a creature turns away; for power it hath,
though thus impelled, to bend aside elsewhere,
(as one may see fire falling from a cloud),
if, by false pleasure drawn, that primal impulse
turn it aside to earth. If well I judge,
no further shouldst thou wonder at thy rising,
than at a stream thou dost, which to its foot
down from a lofty mountain's top descends.
As great a marvel would it be in thee,
if, rid of hindrance, thou hadst sat thee down,

as rest, on earth, would in a living flame."
Then toward the sky she turned her face again.

CANTO XXXIII

The Empyrean. GOD. St. Bernard's Prayer to Mary. The Vision of God. Ultimate Salvation

"O Virgin Mother, Daughter of thy Son,
humbler and loftier than any creature,
eternal counsel's predetermined goal,
thou art the one that such nobility
didst lend to human nature, that its Maker
scorned not to make Himself what He had made.
Within thy womb rekindled was the Love,
through whose warm influence in the eternal Peace
this Flower hath blossomed thus. Here unto us
thou art a noonday torch of Charity;
and down below 'mong mortal men, thou art
a living fount of Hope. Lady, so great
thou art, and hast such worth, that one who longs
for Grace, and unto thee hath not recourse,
wingless would wish to have his longing fly.
Not only doth thy Kindliness give help
to him that asketh it, but many times
it freely runs ahead of his request.
In thee is Mercy, Pity is in thee,
in thee Magnificence, and all there is
of Goodness in a creature meets in thee.
Now doth this man, who from the lowest drain
of the Universe hath one by one beheld,
as far as here, the forms of spirit-life,
beseech thee, of thy grace, for so much strength
that with his eyes he may uplift himself
toward Ultimate Salvation higher still.
And I, who never for mine own sight burned
more than I do for his, offer thee all

my prayers, and pray that they be not too poor,
that thou with thy prayers so dissolve each cloud
of his mortality, that unto him
the Highest Pleasure may unfold Itself.
And furthermore, I pray to thee, O Queen,
who canst whate'er thou wilt, that, after such
a sight, thou keep all his affections sound.
His human promptings let thy care defeat;
see with how many blest ones Beatrice
is clasping for my prayers her hands to thee!"
The eyes belovèd and revered by God,
intent on him who prayed, revealed to us
how grateful unto her are earnest prayers.
Thence they addressed them to the Eternal Light,
wherein it may not be believed the eye
of any creature finds so clear a way.
And I, who to the End of all desires
was drawing near, within me, as I ought,
brought to its goal the ardor of desire.
Bernard was smiling, and was making signs
for me to look on high; but, as he wished,
I was already of mine own accord;
because my sight, as purer it became,
was penetrating more and more the radiance
of that High Light, which of Itself is true.
From this time onward greater was my sight
than is our speech, which yields to such a vision,
and memory also yields to such excess.
And such as he, who seeth in a dream,
and after it, the imprinted feeling stays,
while all the rest returns not to his mind;
even such am I; for almost wholly fades
my vision, yet the sweetness which was born
of it is dripping still into my heart.
Even thus the snow is in the sun dissolved;
even thus the Sibyl's oracles, inscribed
on flying leaves, were lost adown the wind.
O Light Supreme, that dost uplift Thyself
so far from mortal thought, relend my mind

a little of what Thou didst seem to be,
and cause my tongue to be so powerful,
that of Thy Glory it may leave at least
a spark unto the people still to come;
for to my mem'ry if it but a while
return, and speak a little in these lines,
more of Thy Victory will be conceived.

I think the keenness of the living Ray
which I endured would have confounded me,
if from it I had turned away mine eyes.
And I recall that I, because of this,
the bolder was to bear it, till I made
my vision one with Value Infinite.

O the abundant Grace, whereby I dared
to pierce the Light Eternal with my gaze,
until I had therein exhausted sight!

I saw that far within its depths there lies,
by Love together in one volume bound,
that which in leaves lies scattered through the world;
substance and accident, and modes thereof,
fused, as it were, in such a way, that that,
whereof I speak, is but One Simple Light.

This union's general form I think I saw,
since, saying so, I feel that I the more
rejoice. Of more forgetfulness for me
one moment is, than centuries twenty-five
are for the enterprise which once caused Neptune
to wonder at the shadow Argo cast.

My mind, thus wholly in suspense, was gazing
steadfast and motionless, and all intent,
and, gazing, grew enkindled more and more.

Such in that Light doth one at last become,
that one can never possibly consent
to turn therefrom for any other sight;
because the Good, which is the will's real object,
is therein wholly gathered, and, outside,
that is defective which is perfect there.

Ev'n as to what I do remember, mine
will now be shorter than an infant's speech,

who at the breast still bathes his tongue. 'T was not
that there was other than a simple semblance
within the Living Light wherein I gazed,
which always is what It hath been before;
but through my sight, which in me, as I looked,
was gathering strength, because I changed, one sole
appearance underwent a change for me.

Within the Lofty Light's profound and clear
subsistence there appeared to me three Rings,
of threefold color and of one content;
and one, as Rainbow is by Rainbow, seemed
reflected by the other, while the third
seemed like a Fire breathed equally from both.

Oh, how, to my conception, short and weak
is speech! And this, to what I saw, is such,
that it is not enough to call it small.

O Light Eternal, that alone dost dwell
within Thyself, alone dost understand
Thyself, and love and smile upon Thyself,
Self-understanding and Self-understood!

That Circle which appeared to be conceived
within Thyself as a Reflected Light,
when somewhat contemplated by mine eyes,
within Itself, of Its own very color,
to me seemed painted with our Human Form;
whence wholly set upon It was my gaze.

Like the geometer, who gives himself
wholly to measuring the circle, nor,
by thinking, finds the principle he needs;
ev'n such was I at that new sight. I wished
to see how to the Ring the Image there
conformed Itself, and found therein a place;
but mine own wings were not enough for this;
had not my mind been smitten by a flash
of light, wherein what it was willing came.

Here power failed my high imagining;
but, like a smoothly moving wheel, that Love
was now revolving my desire and will,
which moves the sun and all the other stars.

RECOMMENDED RESOURCES

For suggested translations, see *Inferno*.

James Whitbourn, composer, *The Seven Heavens and Other Choral Works*, performed by Cor Cantiamo. This modern composition (2020) presents the seven medieval heavens, related through the life and work of C.S. Lewis.

Michael Ward, *Planet Narnia: The Seven Heavens in the Imagination of C.S. Lewis* and *The Narnia Code* (a shorter distillation of *Planet Narnia*, with an emphasis on the Christian devotional aspect, suitable for younger readers).

C.S. Lewis, *The Discarded Image*, especially the epilogue.

QUESTIONS FOR DISCUSSION

1. Does Dante's heaven attract you? Why or why not? Does it surprise you? If so, in what way?

2. If you could speak with one of the saints in heaven, who would it be? What would you say to that saint, or what would you ask about?

3. Dante uses the imagery of light and movement throughout *Paradiso*. What does that suggest about heaven?

4. Consider St. Bernard's prayer to Mary. How can Mary be both "humbler" and "loftier" than any other creature? Which of these qualities is easier for you to imagine and relate to, and which is harder? Why?

5. How does Dante's vision of the Trinity relate to the Ascension of Christ?

6. What is the effect of Dante's use of references to pagan mythology, as with his invocation of Apollo in canto I?

7. Dante's imagined structure of heaven is based on a characteristically medieval Christian understanding of the world, in which everything (sentient or not) is in relation with God, its Creator, and has a purpose to fulfill. We see this both in Beatrice's explanation of the universe (in canto I) and in the closing line of the poem in canto XXXIII. How does this view of the world challenge the modern materialist view?

USING THE ARTS

1. Have participants create and act out dialogues among other saints (later than Dante's time), following the model of St. Thomas and St. Bonaventure praising St. Francis and St. Dominic.

2. Listen to Gustav Holst's *The Planets*. How does the auditory imagery of each planet, as presented here, relate to the spheres of those planets in *Paradiso*?

3. Consider Dante's images of the seven heavens and/or the mystical rose in *Paradiso*. Have participants illustrate these and discuss the different insights gained from the various images.

Chapter Six
GOING FORWARD

We have explored literature from the pagan myths of the ancient Greeks all the way to Dante's depiction of the beatific vision in *Paradiso*: quite a journey! I hope that you've found these stories and poems to be engaging, intriguing, and enriching for your own faith. The next question is: Where do we go from here? How do we make use of these materials for evangelization and discipleship?

As this book is a resource and guide, not a textbook or a curriculum, you have freedom to use it as you wish, for content and for ideas. But let me offer a few suggestions on how you might make use of *Tales of Faith* in different settings and for different circumstances.

In schools and homeschools

If you are a teacher or a homeschool parent, you can use the introductory essays, the questions for discussion, and the activities to enrich the teaching of any texts from this guide that already appear in your curriculum. Also, look beyond the literature component of your curriculum. If you are doing a unit on ancient Greece or Rome, you could insert discussion of literary works from chapter three into your students' historical studies. Likewise, a unit that touches on medieval Europe or England provides the opportunity to include selected works from chapters four and five. Since *Tales of Faith* includes short excerpts that are suitable for stand-alone use, you can do this easily, even in a single lesson, without adding extensive additional reading to your syllabus.

If you have the opportunity to design or adapt your curriculum, consider including some of these works as main texts, reading them in full and discussing them in depth. I encourage you to select just a handful of texts from *Tales of Faith* to engage with at length. It's better for students to spend more time on a particular literary work, to become comfortable with it and appreciate it, than to dip into a whole slew of them in a shallow manner. If you do use one or more of the texts here as a main text in a class, you will probably have time to go through many or all the discussion questions and activities, which will promote understanding and engagement with the text. The more in-depth discussion questions and some of the art activities are well suited to being adapted as prompts for essays or group projects.

As to which texts to choose for your students: select texts that you, personally, find engaging and that you can have fun with. As the instructor, if you are enthusiastic about the readings, you have a good chance of helping the students to be enthusiastic as well. Of course, you should never expect enthusiasm – or at least, not visible enthusiasm. Teenagers and college students often make a substantial effort to act as if they are bored, because they are painfully self-conscious and afraid of the disapproval of their peers if they should do something so socially unforgivable as to enjoy what they're studying in school. But *your* enthusiasm and interest will not be wasted, and you may well find expressions of sincere engagement on their part coming through in their writing, even if not in person.

In parishes

Literature is very well suited as the material for adult formation programming, whether as 'adult Sunday school' sessions or as seasonal or thematic talks or discussion groups. Since the excerpts provided here are chosen to stand on their own, and are in the public domain, you can make handouts of the relevant texts to distribute to attendees. Furthermore, since many of these works of literature have been depicted beautifully in art, it is relatively easy to create a PowerPoint presentation to provide visuals to accompany your talk.

One option for talks is to make them thematic. Choose a topic and focus each session on a specific literary work from this guide that helps you to show the meaning of a particular Christian concept. For instance, *Pearl* and the Elegies offer a richly meaningful way to explore suffering and loss; the *Odyssey* and the *Aeneid* provide a fresh way to talk about the journey of faith; the Greek gods and Beowulf provide very different pictures of masculinity. Another option is to connect with the liturgical calendar. For instance, "The Dream of the Rood" would be ideal for Lent, Holy Week, or the Feast of the Exaltation of the Holy Cross; *Pearl* and *Paradiso* would be suitable material for the season of Easter. Make sure to bear in mind that your audience won't be familiar with the works in question; it's best for the title and description of the programming to emphasize the Christian content and general theme, so that it's clearly open to everyone.

Discussion groups are another excellent way to make use of this material in a parish setting. A small group of people can meet regularly to read and discuss the texts, meeting at the parish or at participants' homes in person, or having meetings online. In this context, it is possible for people to read the works in full, or at least to read larger sections of them than are possible for a one-off presentation to a group. The discussion questions can be used to start or structure the conversation, allowing plenty of freedom for people to take the discussion in other directions. Groups like this work best if they meet regularly but not too often: once a month or quarterly is a good pace. Thus, people have time to read the material beforehand.

For individuals

There are also many ways to make use of this material for evangelization and discipleship in a more individual and flexible way. To begin with, once you've read and reflected deeply upon a particular work, consider writing a short reflection or meditation on it, using that work of literature to illuminate some aspect of the Christian faith. This reflection would then be suitable for inclusion in your parish's bulletin or newsletter, or shared online, or circulated among friends.

Attentive reading and personal reflection and journaling with the discussion questions will help you better understand, and internalize, the sorts of open-ended and nonthreatening questions that invite deeper engagement.

Most importantly, if you read and reflect on these literary texts, and prayerfully consider the way that they illuminate our understanding of the Christian faith, you will grow as an evangelist. By immersing yourself in works of great beauty, you'll deepen and enrich your own personal understanding of the faith. You will become better at exercising intellectual hospitality; having trained yourself in reading such widely different perspectives as the Greek myths and Dante's *Divine Comedy*, you'll be more able to enter into the point of view of your skeptical or wounded friend. Having carefully worked through challenging poems like *Pearl* and "The Dream of the Rood," you'll have – God willing – more patience with people who are baffled by the strangeness of the Crucifixion and the Resurrection.

May God bless you in your reading, and may the discussions and reflections that arise from these works of literature bear much fruit for Christ's kingdom!

RECOMMENDED RESOURCES

Alan Jacobs, *The Pleasures of Reading in an Age of Distraction* and *Breaking Bread with the Dead.*

C.S. Lewis, *An Experiment in Criticism.*

Leland Ryken, ed. *The Christian Imagination: The Practice of Faith in Literature and Writing.*

Vigen Guroian, *Tending the Heart of Virtue: How Classic Stories Awaken a Child's Moral Imagination.*

Louis Markos, *From Achilles to Christ: Why Christians Should Read the Pagan Classics.*

QUESTIONS FOR DISCUSSION

1. Why is imaginative literature important to the Church?

2. What is a work of fiction, poetry, drama, or creative nonfiction that has had an impact on your Christian faith? Note that it does not have to be written by a Christian. Discuss.

3. What are your current habits of reading? (Consider how often, when, where, and what types of material.) Are you satisfied with these habits? What, if anything, would you like to change?

4. What is intellectual hospitality? Why is it important? Consider the parable of the weeds and the wheat (Matt. 13:24–30). How does this apply to reading literature? How does it operate in discussion?

5. Why is it important for an evangelist to be familiar with a range of literary styles, forms, and periods?

6. Can you recall a time when you learned to like (or appreciate) something that you didn't enjoy at first? What helped you to do that? How can you apply that insight to helping others expand their literary tastes?

7. Some Christians are opposed to reading fiction, viewing it as "lies" and therefore spiritually harmful. Other people (whether Christians or not) view fiction and poetry as simply a waste of time, considering it better to attend to useful nonfiction. How would you respond?

8. Why is patience an essential virtue for evangelists and catechists?

USING THE ARTS

1. Choose one of the literary selections from this book. Read it, then set a timer for ten minutes and draw or doodle for that amount of time as you reflect on what you have read. Then write down any insights you gained from the activity. Ideally, repeat this at least three times, with different texts.

2. Choose one of the literary selections from this book. Read it aloud, preferably to someone else. Then, if you are working with a partner, trade places and have the other person read that text, or another one, aloud. What was it like to experience the text by reading it aloud? By hearing it? How was this different from reading it silently?

Chapter Seven
ADVICE AND PRAYERS FROM THE SAINTS

St. Philip Neri, from *The Maxims and Sayings of St. Philip Neri*[1]

To get good from reading the Lives of the Saints, and other spiritual books, we ought not to read out of curiosity, or skimmingly, but with pauses; and when we feel ourselves warmed, we ought not to pass on, but to stop and follow up the spirit which is stirring in us, and when we feel it no longer then to pursue our reading.

One of the most excellent means of obtaining perseverance is discretion; we must not wish to do everything at once, or become a saint in four days.

St. John Henry Newman's Prayer to St. Philip Neri[2]

Philip, my glorious Advocate, teach me to look at all I see around me after thy pattern as the creatures of God. Let me never forget that the same God who made me made the whole world, and all men and all animals that are in it. Gain me the grace to love all God's works for God's sake, and all men for the sake of my Lord and Saviour who has redeemed them by the Cross. And especially

---

1. *Maxims and Sayings of St. Philip Neri*, trans. F.W. Faber, in *The Life of Saint Philip Neri, Apostle of Rome, and Founder of the Congregation of the Oratory* (London: Thomas Richardson and Son, 1847), 465, 467.

2. "Novena to St. Philip," *Meditations and Devotions* (London: Longmans, Green, and Co., 1907), 105, https://www.newmanreader.org/works/meditations/index.html.

let me be tender and compassionate and loving towards all Christians, as my brethren in grace. And do thou, who on earth was so tender to all, be especially tender to us, and feel for us, bear with us in all our troubles, and gain for us from God, with whom thou dwellest in beatific light, all the aids necessary for bringing us safely to Him and to thee.

St. Thomas Aquinas's Prayer Before Study[3]

Creator of all things, true source of light and wisdom, origin of all being, graciously let a ray of your light penetrate the darkness of my understanding.

Take from me the double darkness in which I have been born, an obscurity of sin and ignorance.

Give me a keen understanding, a retentive memory, and the ability to grasp things correctly and fundamentally.

Grant me the talent of being exact in my explanations and the ability to express myself with thoroughness and charm.

Point out the beginning, direct the progress, and help in the completion.
I ask this through Jesus Christ our Lord.

Amen.

---

3. Adapted from the prayer by St. Thomas Aquinas included in the encyclical *Studiorum Ducem* by Pope Pius XI, 1923.

Acknowledgments

This book comes from years of teaching and talking about literature at various levels and in various contexts: undergraduate and graduate classes, Christian formation for adults and young adults, interviews, and public lectures. As I worked to shape my various notes and ideas into a book, my colleagues at the Word on Fire Institute provided helpful feedback on the concept and early sections of this project. I also wish to give special thanks to Alex Markos for reading the full book in draft and offering valuable comments and suggestions.

I wish particularly to express my appreciation for my students in the MA in Apologetics at Houston Baptist University (both residential and online), especially those who took my Ancient Culture and Philosophy and Medieval Culture and Philosophy classes. They often asked me, "When will you write a book based on your teaching?" This is the book!

Holly Ordway
La Crosse, Wisconsin
Feast of St. Hilda of Whitby